The Rise of Specialist Career Paths in Law Firms

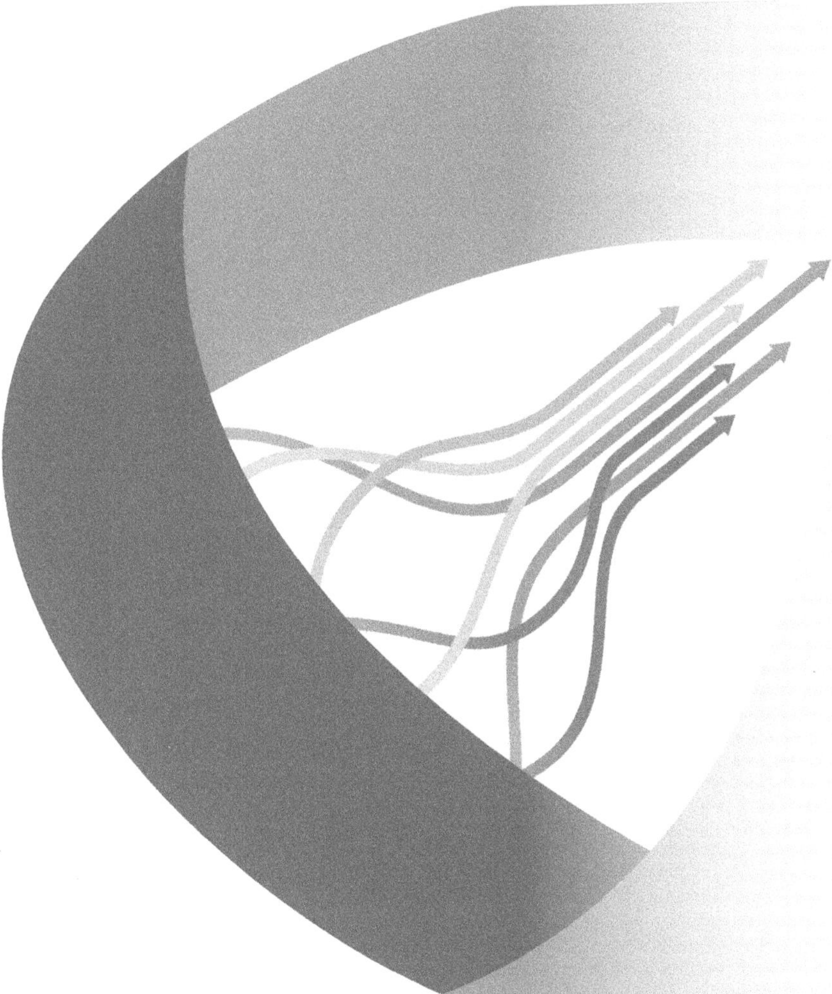

EDITED BY KATERINA MENHENNET

Commissioning editor
Katerina Menhennet

Managing director
Sian O'Neill

The Rise of Specialist Career Paths in Law Firms
is published by

Globe Law and Business Ltd
3 Mylor Close
Horsell
Woking
Surrey GU21 4DD
United Kingdom
Tel: +44 20 3745 4770
www.globelawandbusiness.com

The Rise of Specialist Career Paths in Law Firms

ISBN 9781787428720
EPUB ISBN 9781787428737
Adobe PDF ISBN 9781787428744

Contents

Executive summary

As the evolution of law firms continues, so too does the number of careers available within them. In addition to fee earning, there is now a wider range of roles in law firms than ever before, from those that are more established – such as in knowledge management and risk and compliance – to new and emerging careers such as the ESG lawyer and legal operations professional. These specialist roles are crucial to a law firm's success and there is growing recognition of the respect and value they deserve with increasing numbers gaining positions in senior management.

The Rise of Specialist Career Paths in Law Firms contains chapters focusing on a variety of these careers, written by experts with direct experience exploring and thriving in them. They are in no particular order, except progressing from roles with a longer history in firms to those that are new or developing. With client demands and competition intensifying, as well as extremely high levels of attrition as individuals seek out an improved work–life balance and careers tailored to their skills and interests, these specialist career paths are a vital tool enabling firms to remain competitive and retain both clients and talent. They also provide individual lawyers with the opportunity to find the career that suits them best, allowing them to utilize their unique skillset. Although risk is inherent in any new initiative, it is arguable that not investing in these new roles will be the greater and longer-term risk to a law firm's future success.

In chapter one, Catherine Hart, partner and head of professional support at Digby Brown LLP, examines the role of professional support lawyer (PSL). She introduces the traditional PSL role and how it emerged, then proceeds to analyze how the job has developed over time, encompassing a wider range of responsibilities and increased opportunities. She also examines the core skills that are required to be an effective PSL and why these are important, and how professional support differs from the fee earning role. Catherine argues that the COVID-19 pandemic has reinforced the need for effective professional support as remote and hybrid work continues, and with the expanding and now recognized integral nature of the role to legal teams, demonstrates that a career as a professional support lawyer can be immensely satisfying, varied, and challenging.

Building on learnings in the previous chapter, in chapter two, Lucy Hall, client value lawyer at Shearman & Sterling LLP, discusses the diverse routes a PSL can take over the course of their career. First outlining the different PSL structures found within law firms, ranging from formal career paths with different levels of seniority to flatter structures where everyone's job title is PSL regardless of years of experience and PQE, she then lists some of the other roles PSLs can move in to. She covers senior roles available within law firms and opportunities outside, including in-house, within consultancy practices, and the more recent development of roles in legal tech companies. This chapter shows that PSLs have a wide range of exciting career paths available to them, in a variety of sectors and with the opportunity to advance to a very senior level.

As far as the world is concerned, knowledge management is the bread-and-butter work of any law firm. The understanding and application of legal knowledge is at the heart of every single activity undertaken by lawyers. However, within law firms themselves knowledge management is a specialist role, and one that demands and develops a uniquely versatile skillset. In chapter three, Clare Harman Clark, senior professional support lawyer at Taylor Wessing LLP, discusses the role of the legal knowledge manager in today's law firm and how this has developed from the traditional PSL role of the 1990s. Clare explores the three "suns" a legal knowledge manager revolves around, namely bolstering organizational capacity, bridging the technology gap, and encouraging and empowering people. She then concludes with a look to the future, and the observation that despite the challenges, it is an exciting time to be in knowledge management, and that today's knowledge managers have a crucial part to play in the evolution of law firms.

Although originating in the 1970s, there has been an exponential growth in the number of pro bono roles in recent years as law firms seek to maximize their societal impact and gain the full benefits of their pro bono practices. In our next chapter, Amy Grunske, head of international pro bono, sustainability and community responsibility at Orrick, provides guidance on the pro bono opportunities available and why this role can be a wonderful career step for any lawyer with a passion for social justice and a thirst for variety in their day-to-day work. She explores the tasks and responsibilities pro bono roles entail, the skills needed to be successful in them, and what a typical day as a pro bono lawyer might look like, with contributions and insights from active pro bono professionals all over the world. Additionally, there is information on the support available for pro bono professionals, and advice on how those interested might pursue a career in this space.

Further career opportunities can be found in a law firm's risk and compliance department. In chapter five, Rebecca Atkinson, director of risk and compliance at Howard Kennedy, firstly provides a sample of the risk and compliance areas of practice, before looking at the different structures that can be found in law firms' risk and compliance departments, reflecting the different levels of seniority and potential career progression routes. She then goes on to outline the different roles that exist, including those required by law, what each of these entails, and how the roles interact with one another. Rebecca also reveals the skills and attributes needed for roles in risk and compliance, the knowledge and qualifications required, and courses, training, and materials that are available to support this. Chapter five concludes with a view of what the future looks like for risk and compliance teams in law firms.

We all know that clients are the lifeblood of every legal firm. This brings into focus the need for every law firm to focus on and prioritize business development. How do you embed a culture of business development throughout your firm? How do you put in place structures to allow those within the firm with a talent and flair for business development to carve out a career path focused on just that? Most importantly, how do you ensure that those within your firm who dedicate their careers to bringing in business for their fellow lawyers do not end up labelled as "non-fee earners" or considered a "cost"? Chapter six by Anne Macdonald, partner and head of business development at Harper Macleod LLP, explores each of these pertinent questions as well as considering the benefits of bringing legal experience to business development and providing guidance on how firms can best structure their business development team to allow all to flourish. With insights from some of the early movers in legal business development, this chapter showcases that a career in legal business development is a fantastic career choice for lawyers and for some may well prove more fulfilling than the traditional career path.

Law is a people business, and chapter seven, by Rachel Brushfield, founder of EnergiseLegal, explores the shifting sands in talent management as a result of the COVID-19 pandemic, how it has gained HR and talent professionals the recognition they deserve, and the plethora of opportunities now available in this space. She outlines the different roles individuals can take up, as well as how to identify the right one for you, and different qualifications for and routes into talent management. The current and future emerging skills needed to perform talent roles are also examined, and practical tips and guidance are provided for how to market, brand, and network yourself into the talent management space, including a case study of the author's own successful career pivot. "HR has arrived!" Rachel concludes, demonstrating that working in HR and talent management is an exciting and ever evolving opportunity to be right at the heart of a law firm: its people.

Chapter eight focuses on the role of communications in law firms. Hayley Geffin, head of communications at Mishcon de Reya, outlines how communications has changed in the sector over the last several decades, from the PR and media landscape to a focus on internal comms and engagement with the firm's people. She highlights the current, varying responsibilities of communications professionals today and the centrality of brand to their role. Hayley also provides guidance on growing a strong communications team, demonstrating how experiences and skills from different sectors can be invaluable to a law firm, and concludes with a bright outlook that the sky is the limit for professionals who are not lawyers in law firms. With their help, firms can demonstrate operational excellence in their own business, helping them stand out to clients in the competitive legal market.

It is an exciting time in the legal industry, with many opportunities to innovate. Innovation in the business of law and how law firms provide legal services to clients is currently where most opportunities lie, and where Amy Monaghan, director of client innovation at Perkins Coie, focuses her practice. In this chapter, Amy draws links from her unique career path to her everyday work as a legal innovator, and the skills she learnt along the way that have proved invaluable for a career in innovation. She also provides an overview of the different and wide-ranging areas of legal her role touches and how she and her team engage in cross-functional collaboration to promote change. Chapter nine closes with a discussion of the changing legal industry and some examples of opportunities that are opening up in the legal innovation space to meet these changes, for example product designers and relationship specialists, reflecting the crucial role relationships play in legal innovation.

Chapter ten, written by Tammy Heydenrych, managing consultant, and Tom Evans, legal operations consultant at Norton Rose Fulbright, examines careers in legal operations. They begin by explaining what legal operations is, and how it means different things to different people, as well as wider trends relating to the growth in legal operations and what outcomes legal operations look to achieve. They then move on to the evolving legal operations landscape and the roles and skills that are emerging in the industry. A few prominent examples of these specialties are explored, including legal project management and external resource management, and the chapter concludes with advice on building a career in legal operations, with a reminder that with the diverse range of disciplines and skills involved, it is a continuous improvement mindset, rather than a specific skillset, that is crucial for success in this arena.

Our next chapter takes a closer look at the emerging career path of the legal engineer. Nina Gramcko, lawyer and manager at PwC Legal Germany, firstly covers what a legal engineer does, including legal service process analysis and improvement, implementing procured technology, and deploying customized technology. All of this requires a thorough understanding of the legal sector and legal services, as well as the ability to translate the requirements from law to tech. Nina identifies these as the key skills of a legal engineer and explores others that they require, in particular communication and the ability to think holistically, analytically, and in an agile way. Chapter 11 also assists law firms in deciding whether this role should be created in their organization, by analysing whether their needs can be fulfilled by an engineer, and what law firms need to implement this role successfully.

"ESG is everywhere", says Claire Shasha, lawyer and ESG advocate and author of our next chapter, and the legal profession is no exception. In chapter 12, Claire provides a brief background to ESG and outlines the key emerging trends, including the rise of regulation and reporting and the increased pressure from consumers and stakeholders. Although ESG roles and service offerings are at a relatively early stage of development across the legal industry, Claire discusses the roles that are becoming increasingly available both in-house and in private practice, as well as practical steps lawyers can take if they wish to pivot their career and develop their expertise in this space, whether within a law firm or in other companies. ESG is an area that will only continue to grow in significance, and a lawyer's unique skillset means they are perfectly placed to help companies and firms achieve their ESG goals and have an important role to play in the overall ESG agenda.

The final chapter by Rebecca Holdredge, director of knowledge management at Levenfeld Pearlstein, looks to the future of legal career paths, specifically the growing trend of "hyperspecialization". As the legal industry continues its digital transformation – as evidenced by more mature software companies – hyperspecialization will occur, whereby the traditional attorney role is broken down into smaller and smaller tasks, creating new specialized legal careers and enhancing efficiency and work quality. In chapter 13, Rebecca explains the concept of hyperspecialization and how this occurs in the context of the Digital Revolution, as well as what this means for the legal industry. As shown throughout this book the concept of specialization has already increased the availability of careers for those with a legal background, and to conclude Rebecca demonstrates that as hyperspecialization continues to permeate the legal industry, more and more new roles will emerge, including those that do not even yet exist.

About the authors

Rebecca Atkinson is director of risk and compliance at Howard Kennedy. She leads the firm's internal risk and compliance function and sets the related strategy. Rebecca is a skilled risk and compliance professional with over a decade of experience ensuring businesses are compliant. She is the firm's compliance officer for legal practice, money laundering reporting officer, money laundering compliance officer, anti-bribery officer, and whistleblowing officer. She additionally holds the position of data protection officer alongside head of technology and security Jonathan Freedman. Rebecca is a barrister (non-practicing), New York attorney and solicitor of England and Wales. Rebecca has authored two books (*Assessing and Addressing Risk and Compliance in Your Law Firm* and *Financial Crime A Compliance Manual*) and regularly produces written content for compliance publications, as well as *Practice Notes for Practical Law Company*. Rebecca sits on the Board for the Law Society Legal Compliance Bulletin and is a Member of the Law Society Regulatory Processes Committee.

Founder of EnergiseLegal (1997), **Rachel Brushfield** is "The Talent Liberator", with over 30 years' experience. Her career heritage is in marketing and brand strategy and communications for design, advertising, and innovation agencies, including WPP. She is an experienced coach and published author in talent management, professional development, work life balance, career management, marketing yourself, and gender balance for the Law Society, Ark Group and Globe Law and Business (in association with The International Bar Association (IBA)). Rachel features on LexisNexis "Meet the expert" page and was a judge in the Marketing and Communications category of the 2019 Law Society Excellence Awards. She is co-founder of the network PWHub for senior employed women in Oxfordshire, with portfolio careers a specialism. Rachel has supported the Law Society Returners course for over a decade. Her portfolio career currently includes a part-time contract for the charity ProAge – age inclusive intelligence for managers and leaders for productive and high-performance intergenerational working.

Tom Evans is a legal operations consultant and an alumni of NRF Transform's Business and Legal Operations Graduate Scheme. Tom has worked across an extensive range of legal operations disciplines including resource management, innovation and legal product development, supporting both Norton Rose Fulbright as well as its clients. Tom now advises solely on helping in-house legal departments to improve the way that they operate, and has worked on projects spanning strategic planning, technology implementation, external resource management, and document automation. Tom's experience has covered teams of varying sizes, across energy, financial services, and heavy industry clients. Having previously worked as a paralegal, case manager, and a recruitment consultant, Tom is passionate about promoting alternative career paths in the legal industry, and the value that novel skillsets can bring to the legal industry as a whole.

Hayley Geffin is head of communications at Mishcon de Reya. She joined the firm in 2010 having worked in publishing and editorial roles prior to that. She has extensive experience of advising on corporate communications and works across public relations, editorial, marketing and brand campaigns, and social media. She also leads on internal communications. She works alongside lawyers to provide clients with communications advice including in relation to crisis communications, group actions, and crowdfunding. Hayley was part of the team that brought the Article 50 legal challenge on behalf of Gina Miller in 2016, handling communications and media for both Mrs Miller and the firm.

Nina Gramcko is a lawyer and manager at PwC Legal Germany. In the NewLaw team, she helps create business solutions for clients that integrate people, technology, and processes. She graduated from Berlin's Humboldt University and also studied at the University of Málaga. She passed the bar in 2016. She started her career helping to create a new legal and digital world in 2010, when she joined flightright GmbH at the dawn of legal tech and alternative legal services in Germany as head of operations. Before joining PwC Germany she worked as a lawyer and legal engineer at an international law firm and consultant for lawtech implementations and legal project management and legal process management.

Amy Grunske is the head of international pro bono, sustainability and community responsibility at Orrick based in London, leading the pro bono practice in the firm's 12 offices across the UK, Continental Europe, and

Asia. She builds strong partnerships and networks across sectors to collaboratively develop high impact pro bono projects that use the law, policy, and advocacy as tools for social change and development in areas such as access to justice, human rights, and rule of law. Amy is an Australian-qualified lawyer, holds graduate and post-graduate degrees in the areas of law, human rights, and psychology, and has worked in the pro bono sector for over a decade.

Lucy Hall is the client value lawyer in the project development and finance EMEA team at Shearman & Sterling LLP, based in London. This is a strategic role in which she is responsible for knowledge management for the team. She writes and delivers internal and client training, and is heavily involved in legal technology and process improvement. She also undertakes significant projects and develops strategies in certain key sectors, such as energy innovation and hydrogen. Lucy supports the PDF EMEA team and works closely with the client value team, knowledge and research team, legal project management team, and legal technology team globally. She authored the chapter on "What tech is best?" in *The Evolving Role of the Professional Support Lawyer* (Ark Publishing, now part of Globe Law and Business, 2018). Lucy is an experienced knowledge professional and has previously worked as a senior professional support lawyer at Eversheds Sutherland, Hogan Lovells, and Mayer Brown over the past five years. Prior to that, Lucy trained and qualified into the banking and finance team at Mayer Brown in London and worked as a fee earner there for ten years.

Clare Harman Clark is a senior professional support lawyer at Taylor Wessing LLP, building on a legal career that began with nearly a decade practicing commercial property law at Clifford Chance and a period at Russell Cooke. Honing a professional focus on knowledge management, she is also the chair of the Law Society Property Section, the national community for commercial and residential practitioners, and has recently taken up a role on the editorial board of the *Landlord and Tenant Review*. She also works as a guest lecturer on the LPC course at the University of Westminster. Before retraining as a lawyer, Clare worked as a journalist, on both private B2B publications and within a government press office, and still regularly publishes articles in national and trade press.

Catherine Hart is a qualified solicitor who practices in Scotland and has been in the profession for 30 years. She worked as a fee earner in litigation teams for the first half of her career, but the direction of her career changed around 15 years ago when she took up a role as a professional support lawyer. She worked for Biggart Ballie LLP (now DWF LLP) for seven years, before joining Digby Brown LLP, a firm that specializes in personal injury claims. Catherine is now a partner and head of professional support at Digby Brown LLP. She has spoken at a number of events about the importance of professional support, a topic she is passionate about, and has also written about the role. Catherine has been a tutor and senior tutor on several courses on the Diploma in Professional Legal Practice at Glasgow University for over a decade and is still involved in the Diploma in a non-teaching role. She is also a vice chair of the Scottish Solicitors' Discipline Tribunal and has an interest in regulation and compliance.

Tammy Heydenrych is a managing consultant within Norton Rose Fulbright's legal operations consulting practice. A first of its kind within a global law firm, legal operations consulting sits within NRF Transform – the firm's technology and innovation program – and helps GCs and in-house legal teams optimize the delivery of legal services to their organizations. Tammy was formerly the group company secretary and senior legal advisor for Zurich Insurance's Southern African operations, overseeing corporate governance across multiple jurisdictions and delivering various strategic projects within both legal and compliance and across the broader business. Tammy began her career as a litigation and commercial lawyer, practicing across areas such as insurance, banking, and constitutional law, representing the interests of political parties, government departments, and corporate entities. With over 18 years' experience within professional services, corporate and start-up environments, Tammy has extensive expertise in corporate governance, strategy formulation, operational design, and delivering business transformation projects. She holds an MBA, an LLB, is a chartered company secretary and certified project manager.

As the director of knowledge management at Levenfeld Pearlstein, **Rebecca Holdredge** is responsible for guiding the firm's vision with respect to knowledge management and innovation. In her role, Rebecca manages the firm's knowledge sharing and collaboration tools internally and externally and works closely with attorneys and other business professionals to address unmet client needs, streamline operations, and leverage data to optimize client value. Given her unique background as an attorney and actuary, Rebecca's passion lies at the intersection of business and law, helping law firms reimagine how they deliver legal services by creatively blending change management, product management, and user experience techniques. With over 20 years of experience in professional services, she often lectures and publishes on topics including knowledge management, innovation, law firm operations and economics, pricing, and design thinking. Rebecca graduated from Tulane University Law School and holds a bachelor's degree in mathematics and computer science from Washington University in St. Louis. She co-founded a non-profit, BluePrint Legal Solutions, whose mission is to bridge the gap between technology, process improvement, and access to justice by helping non-profit legal service providers improve the quality and efficiency of their services.

Anne Macdonald is an equity partner with Harper Macleod LLP, a full service independent Scottish law firm. Anne is the head of the business development team and has 15 years' experience of business development in the legal profession, specializing in client engagement and development strategies to secure sustainable relationships for the firm. Anne has a particular focus on inter-law firm relationships and client referrals and set up a Scottish legal referral and support network called HM Connect in 2008. HM Connect has over 390 small to medium-sized Scottish law firm members that refer clients to Harper Macleod on a daily basis. Anne is responsible for managing global law firm relationships and creating best friend relationships around the world. Anne is a senior officer of the IBA Law Firm Management Committee (LFMC) and past chair of the business development and marketing sub-committee of the LFMC. Closer to home, Anne served for six years as a council member of the Law Society of Scotland and is the convenor of the Law Society of Scotland client protection sub-committee.

Amy Monaghan is director of client innovation at Perkins Coie and serves as co-chair of the firmwide innovation working group. In her role, she collaborates with clients, attorneys, and firm leadership to further strategic client-driven innovation objectives, including new legal service delivery models and corresponding firm business models. Amy leads a growing team of legal innovators and technologists and has been integrally involved in the firm's participation in innovative law school programs, such as the Institute for the Future of the Law Profession. Amy frequently speaks and writes on legal innovation topics and volunteers with the International Legal Technology Association (ILTA) as team lead for the knowledge management and marketing content team. She has been named a "Young Professional to Watch" by ILTA for two consecutive years and co-led the project team that won ILTA's 2020 "Transformative Project of the Year". Amy graduated from

Chicago-Kent College of Law in 2013 and holds a fine arts degree from the School of the Art Institute of Chicago. Outside of work, she continues her visual arts practice and enjoys exploring the Pacific Northwest with her husband and rescue greyhounds. Amy is passionate about using creative problem solving to help improve legal work and client service, as well as empowering everyone to be innovative.

Claire Shasha is a legal, risk, compliance, and governance expert who is passionate about ESG and D&I. Claire holds a master's degree in psychology and has been a qualified solicitor for over 13 years. She has lived and worked in the Middle East and the US and has ten years' experience in the financial services sector. Claire has worked as in-house counsel for Sun Life Financial of Canada, Vitality, and Bupa and has held a variety of roles including head of legal, head of risk, head of legal risk and most recently ESG manager. She co-ran a grass roots diversity and inclusion forum for Bupa, which held events including "How to have Compassionate Conversations with Dr Nancy Dome" and "Building Resilience with Katie Piper". Claire is an avid ballroom dancer and has competed at Blackpool. She also enjoys walking and is embarking on walking the entire Camino de Santiago pilgrims trail in 2022.

Chapter 1:
The role of the professional support lawyer

By Catherine Hart, partner and head of professional support, Digby Brown LLP

Introduction

Before moving into professional support, I spent over a decade as a litigation fee earner. While I enjoyed elements of the job and gained satisfaction from a successful court appearance or achieving an especially good result for a client, I was not certain that this was what I wanted to do for the rest of my career. I worked part-time while my family was young at a time when this was much more unusual than it is now, and working part-time was generally seen as demonstrating a lack of interest in career progression.

Everything changed when, in 2007, I saw an advert for a professional support lawyer (PSL) in the litigation department of a long-established Scottish firm. At that stage, I had not heard of the role and knew no one working in professional support, but curiosity led me to apply and by the end of the interview, I knew that it was a role I wanted. This was further reinforced by discussing the role with an existing PSL who worked in another practice area of the business. Her enthusiasm for the role and description of what her job entailed excited me and, although the focus of our work was likely to be different, I felt that a role in professional support would play to my strengths and that I was ready for the challenge that a change of direction would bring. I was delighted to be offered the job – and I haven't looked back since! Having now spent around half of my career in professional support, I still thoroughly enjoy my job and I am passionate about promoting this career route.

The "traditional" professional support role and how this emerged

At the outset, it may be helpful to explain that the term "professional support" is not one that everyone favors – I think largely due to a perception that suggests a non-legal or secondary role. In some businesses, the role is referred to as "practice development", "knowledge development", or even "know-how", but I have always been comfortable with the designation of professional support lawyer or PSL.

The PSL role has evolved considerably since it emerged in the 1990s, originally in large London firms. As solicitors faced increasing pressure to generate fees, they had less time to devote to other aspects of practice such as developing precedents or undertaking research. It was recognized that there would be benefit in experienced solicitors taking a step back from fee earning to provide support to colleagues by focusing on the non-fee earning aspects of the job. The role is now very well established, with larger firms often having teams of PSLs in various departments and in some cases a distinct career structure for their PSLs, with the opportunity to attain partnership, or a partner equivalent level.[1]

Originally, the PSL role was viewed as one largely taken on by women, perhaps looking for a less demanding, part-time position and better work life balance after having a family. Unfortunately, this sometimes resulted in the role being seen as having limited career prospects but, over time, perceptions have changed and professional support is now seen as a positive career option, with many solicitors working full-time in a professional support role.

PSLs can be found in most of the traditional practice areas such a corporate, litigation, and real estate, and there are also professional support roles in what might be considered more niche areas, such as tax and IP/IT.

Central to the vast majority of professional support roles is knowledge management (KM). KM is essentially the creation, gathering, and sharing of information in various forms. Formal or explicit knowledge can take the form of briefing notes, research, and case updates, whereas tacit knowledge is much harder to capture as it is gained through experience, making it more difficult to share. A PSL can play a significant role in both promoting and developing a culture in which sharing knowledge and experience is encouraged. This is vital in legal practice as it allows fee earners to learn from more experienced colleagues, encourages consistency of practice, and avoids the need to "re-invent the wheel". Many PSLs will be responsible for maintaining a central knowledge bank and, to be of value, the content must be regularly reviewed and developed so that users can rely on this as accurate and up to date.

Fee earners need to be aware of developments in their area of practice, but finding the time to do this can be a challenge and part of a PSL's role will often be providing briefing notes or training on relevant case law, legislation, and changes to keep the fee earners up to speed.

How the role has developed

Just as the perception of the professional support role has changed over the last three decades, so too has the nature of the role. Originally, professional support was seen largely as a "back room" function with little or no interaction with clients and a focus on maintaining precedents, undertaking research, and delivering training.

While these aspects still form part of the role of many PSLs, the other areas in which PSLs might become involved are many and varied, which means that it can be difficult to define what the "typical" role of a PSL entails, as much depends on the priorities and requirements of the particular practice area and its fee earners.

Many PSLs now become involved in cross-departmental or business-wide initiatives such as IT projects and the development of consistent practice policies. The PSL's knowledge, not only of the law, but also of day-to-day practice, can provide valuable input into firm-wide initiatives and projects. Their involvement in such projects provides a link between the fee earners and other parts of the business, and helps to establish the PSL as an integral and valued member, not only of their immediate team, but also of the wider business.

This leads on to another way in which the role has developed as there are increasing opportunities to become involved in other aspects of the business, rather than simply advising on the law in a particular practice area. When our business decided to undertake preparation for the introduction of the GDPR (now the UK GDPR) in 2018, I saw this as an opportunity to develop my knowledge in a new area. I knew little about data protection and there was no one else with the necessary breadth of knowledge, so I stepped up and offered to lead the project. This was very time consuming combined with my existing workload, but I have now established myself as the "go to" person for advice and guidance on data protection, not only among the fee earners, but in other business teams.

PSLs are increasingly taking on tasks with a client-facing element. They may be involved in delivering training to clients or in contributing to tender submissions and pitches. Clients usually look for added value and a strong professional support/knowledge management provision demonstrates that the business is serious about ensuring that fee earners are kept up to date and have the necessary resources to work efficiently. In addition, clients may be able to benefit directly, for example, by having access to the services of the PSL and to know-how that they have produced.

Whereas in the past, PSLs would draft an article or opinion piece that would be published in the name of a fee earner, often a partner or department head, increasing recognition of the role and the expertise that goes with it means that PSLs are more likely to publish articles in their own name or to be credited in collaboration with fee earning colleagues.

The skills required to be an effective PSL

Traditionally, professional support roles were undertaken by more senior lawyers with years of fee earning experience but, increasingly, there are roles open to more junior lawyers (fewer than five years' post qualifying experience), particularly in businesses where there is a team of PSLs of differing seniority supporting a particular practice area. This makes sense as it allows the work of the professional support team to be allocated to those best placed to deal with it and there is no doubt that the skills required to be an effective PSL can be developed by working with more senior colleagues.

However, for a PSL supporting a team on their own, in my view a reasonable amount of fee earning experience is important because it gives the PSL a practical perspective and an awareness of fee earners' requirements and the pressures that they face. This can help in understanding what the fee earners require and what will work best from their perspective. For example, a guidance note on a new piece of legislation that explains how changes are likely to work in practice and their impact on the fee earners' day-to-day work will be much more useful than a note simply summarizing the main provisions. Fee earners may also be more likely to trust the opinion of someone who has practical fee earning experience when it comes to seeking advice or a sounding board on day-to-day aspects of practice.

Aside from knowledge of the relevant areas(s) of law, to be effective in a professional support role, there are some core skills that are essential, as outlined below.

Excellent communication skills

The ability to provide accurate and clear information, often concisely, both orally and in writing, is crucial. Whether preparing content for a knowledge bank, writing a briefing note on a new piece of legislation, or drafting an article for the firm's website, it is important that PSLs can express themselves clearly and ensure that the key points are conveyed correctly.

PSLs may be expected to deliver presentations or training, either to their own team or to clients and, again, strong communication skills are essential.

Analytical skills

In most businesses, there is no shortage of legal information available to fee earners, but the pressure on their time can make absorbing the relevant aspects and assessing their effect on day-to-day practice challenging. This is where the strength of a PSL should lie. They should have the time to read and distil the knowledge available so that they can provide the fee earners with the key points affecting their practice area and the information that is important to them.

Horizon scanning is an increasing part of the role, especially for those at a more senior level, and combining legal knowledge with an awareness and understanding of the sector in which their team operates is important in assessing future legal developments and how these are likely to impact the work of the team and the advice given to clients.

Flexibility

PSLs need to be prepared to put aside what they have planned to do if something needs to be dealt with urgently, for example a request for research required for an imminent court hearing. While it can be frustrating to have to re-focus priorities, this flexibility is essential in the role if the team is to be supported effectively.

A "can do" attitude

To be successful in a professional support role, a strong desire to help people is very important. When a fee earner approaches a PSL with an issue or problem, the last thing they want to hear is "that's not something that I can help with". Taking a positive approach to requests or issues means that the PSL is far more likely to be appreciated and to be given the opportunity to become involved in more wide ranging work.

Proactive/problem solving

Following on from the previous point, effective PSLs are solutions-driven and can consider an issue and come up with ways of addressing it. Identifying areas where support is required and how to add value is crucial, as any initiative that can help the fee earners to work more productively will be appreciated. Creativity is also necessary to come up with solutions that will work in practice. This may be identifying someone external to deliver training to cover a gap in the fee earner's knowledge or creating and maintaining an easily accessible database of information.

Effective time management and self-motivation

Effective time management is crucial to the role. PSLs are often given work from a number of different sources and assessing what should be given priority and the timescale in which a piece of work can reasonably be delivered is essential.

Whether working as a team or as a solo PSL, it can be challenging to find the motivation to work on some tasks, particularly where there is no defined timescale or schedule for completion. It can be easy to let tasks drift, so the ability to stay motivated is definitely vital. Motivation can also come from being proactive and seeking out opportunities to add value.

How professional support differs from the more traditional legal role of fee earning

Some differences are obvious – PSLs are not fee earners and do not have their own cases or transactions to progress. Their performance is rarely assessed in terms of KPIs and the majority do not time record, although I have come across businesses that expect their PSLs to record their time and have specific time codes to allow for this. If time spent on a task related to a particular file is recorded against that file, this may be of benefit to the PSL as it is a tangible measure of the value that they have added to a case or transaction.

PSLs do not face the pressure of complying with court timetables and transaction deadlines. They do not have clients pressing for progress or regular updates, although it can be useful to think of fee earning colleagues as clients in terms of the importance of meeting their support needs and expectations.

Being a PSL often involves attending regular meetings, perhaps not with clients, but team meetings with fee earners and, where relevant, with other PSLs or those involved in the KM function, as well as with colleagues working in other areas of the business.

The professional support role can also offer flexibility, as there is often scope to work part-time and it lends itself to working at home, although spending time in the office is important to maintain the PSL's profile among the fee earners. Although fee earners are also being offered more opportunities to work from home, especially in light of the COVID-19 pandemic, many businesses still expect fee earners to be present in the office. While working part-time as a fee earner has certainly become more widespread, this is not always easy in practice due to the pressures of transaction deadlines and court dates.

Although PSLs do not generate fees directly, it is now more widely recognized that their work contributes to the generation of fees by allowing fee earners to spend more of their time focusing on billable work and supporting them to work more efficiently and effectively. However, it is often difficult to identify a tangible measure of the results and effect of work undertaken and this is something that those in professional support can find challenging.

As has already been mentioned, increasingly professional support is moving away from a "back room" function, with PSLs having direct contact with clients, for example though a tender process or presenting training.

Particularly at a more senior level, increasingly PSLs are expected to have an understanding of the overall strategy of the business and to address the ways in which they can support their team in delivering that strategy. I am expected to produce an annual business plan for my team setting out what are we going to do in the coming year to support the business's strategy. This can be very useful as it gives my team a focus for the year ahead and allows me to demonstrate the value we have added over the past year in fulfilling elements of the plan.

While the pressures and focus may be different, in my experience, a role in professional support can be just as demanding as one in fee earning.

Conclusion

Professional support is an area where there will continue to be opportunities for those who want to pursue an alternative career route to fee earning. There was a period recently during which some concern was expressed in the PSL community about the development of artificial intelligence (AI) and the extent to which this might reduce the need for professional support. However, this has not proven to be a significant threat to the role and although there are areas in which AI can assist the work of lawyers, I would argue that this cannot replace the value that an effective PSL adds as a central point of contact to encourage the sharing of knowledge and best practice.

The past couple of years living with COVID-19 have, in my view, reinforced the need for effective professional support as colleagues work remotely or move to a hybrid model and therefore have less opportunity to learn from time spent with more senior colleagues in the office environment. This makes effective support and accessible and up-to-date resources all the more necessary.

As well as the more traditional elements of professional support, such as maintaining precedents and delivering training, there are opportunities to develop new skills and knowledge and to work on cross-department projects.

While previously there was a tendency to see the role as somehow less significant than fee earning, this is no longer the case. An effective PSL will be seen as integral to the team that they support, their views will be respected by colleagues, and their contribution to profitability will be recognized and valued.

I would highly recommend a career as a professional support lawyer. It can be an immensely satisfying role involving varied and challenging work and opportunities.

References

1. See chapter two: Career paths for professional support lawyers for more information.

Chapter 2:
Career paths for professional support lawyers

By Lucy Hall, client value lawyer, Shearman & Sterling LLP

Diverse routes a professional support lawyer (PSL) can take over his or her career

As experienced, dynamic, adaptable, and proactive senior lawyers, PSLs can pursue a range of paths over the course of their careers. PSLs can seek careers within a law firm, in-house, at legal knowledge providers such as LexisNexis and Thomson Reuters, within the legal tech industry, and by developing their own consultancy services. The opportunities are endless and the range of career choices for PSLs is exciting as so many new avenues have developed in recent years.

PSL career structures in law firms

Some law firms have highly defined career paths for PSLs. Usually, the entry level for a PSL is a lawyer who is at least five years' qualified. However, many PSLs pursue this career path having fee earned for ten to 20 or more years and worked as senior lawyers and partners with demonstrable expertise and knowledge, and are critical to their team's strategic growth and performance. In Magic Circle law firms and some US law firms PSLs can progress to senior PSL, counsel PSL, and even partner PSL, the more experienced they become. There are clear objectives for PSLs to reach the next level of promotion. It is wonderful to see that the value of the PSL is so highly regarded that there are now several counsel PSLs and partner PSLs in high caliber law firms.

Regional law firms in the UK have similar career structures such as PSL, senior associate PSL, principal associate PSL, and legal director PSL. The career path is defined at each level and PSLs will progress through the law firm following this structure.

Other law firms refer to their PSLs as knowledge development lawyers (KDLs). In this career structure there is a KDL, principal KDL, and an associate director KDL. In the US, the role is often referred to as a knowledge management attorney (KMA) and senior KMA.

A new development is the title of client value lawyer, which is considered to be an elevated PSL role at US law firms. This role focuses on the legal tech and innovation aspects within a law firm, as well as performing some of the traditional elements of a PSL role. A client value lawyer can either sit within a legal department of a law firm or can instead be solely focused on managing and delivering a specific global project. It is exciting that this new job title has evolved and highlights how important providing the best client value is to law firms.

This development of new and evolving job titles for PSLs demonstrates that law firms are fully invested in offering this career path to lawyers. The PSL role is recognized as having its own distinct career structure and is a viable and attractive option for experienced lawyers who choose to pursue this career path.

Flat structure of PSLs in law firms

Some law firms have instead decided to retain one title of PSL regardless of the level of qualification from six+ years PQE to 25+ years PQE. This creates a clear identity and community of PSLs but lateral hire lawyers from other law firms with different PSL structures may not initially realize the seniority of the PSL in their team. It is debatable whether PSLs prefer a unifying job title or would instead like some degree of hierarchy and formal career progression to reflect their seniority and experience.

Senior roles for PSLs within law firms

Head of knowledge/head of central knowledge management/head of knowledge and collaboration technologies

Head of knowledge is an interesting role, which some PSLs pursue. They may lead a knowledge team that encompasses library and information services, research, and the knowledge and content and systems team, which manage current awareness tools. This role may also involve coordinating a law firm's strategy around its client-facing knowledge offering. They may have overall responsibility for training programs for junior lawyers.

The head of knowledge may work closely with PSLs to develop a wide range of key strategic projects and initiatives involving the delivery of excellent client service and creating a culture of knowledge sharing across the law firm.

Chief knowledge officer/chief knowledge and client value officer/director of professional support/global director of knowledge/global chief knowledge officer

These are all very prestigious senior roles within law firms. These roles are taken up by experienced lawyers who have also worked as senior PSLs for numerous years or by partners who have moved into the area of knowledge management and the business of a law firm.

They usually report to the COO and/or the managing partner and have the responsibility of delivering the law firm's knowledge, innovation, and information strategy. There will be a strong focus on client service. In addition, they may lead the law firm's innovation team and develop the technology, process optimization, and project management aspects of a law firm. They might also identify opportunities for the firm to collaborate with clients to develop their client's operational and strategic goals.

In this role, they may lead the global knowledge management department, which could consist of professional support lawyers, library and research, knowledge systems, records and information, conflicts and new business intake, and governance and compliance teams. The role can be very broad, and the focus is to develop and implement efficient processes that enable the law firm to use its knowledge to benefit its clients worldwide.

Generally, this type of role will be leading a global team of PSLs and knowledge departments across multiple offices around the world. This role exists in most of the Magic Circle, Silver Circle, and US law firms and most major law firms throughout the UK. It is an excellent senior management role that highlights the importance of knowledge management within law firms.

Other senior roles within law firms

Some PSLs pursue other senior roles within law firms, such as senior in-house counsel, assistant general counsel, and deputy general counsel. These roles focus on the compliance and risk management in law firms. They are critical to law firms to ensure that they are complying with their risk and professional and legal duties.

Senior in-house counsel is a role for experienced PSLs who will support the business of the law firm in the global projects and risk management team. They might also support specific departments within a law firm. They may have responsibility for the law firm's legal and regulatory data compliance across its international practice.

Deputy general counsel or assistant general counsel are usually career options for those PSLs who have pursued roles in the risk and compliance aspects of a law firm. In these roles, they generally advise on general risk and compliance matters and may focus on resolving conflicts of interest and ethics questions and sanctions.

In Magic Circle law firms, the role of deputy general counsel may involve being responsible for developing the strategy and management of the in-house legal department. which provides in-house legal and regulatory advice to the firm in all jurisdictions on legal matters and risk management issues.

Roles for PSLs outside law firms

Senior roles in-house

Large businesses, commercial banks, and media and telecommunications companies also employ PSLs within their in-house legal departments, which can often be the size of small law firms with 150 lawyers or more. They will perform a similar function as PSLs in law firms and will manage legal queries, organize external training from law firms, develop the knowledge strategy, and monitor legal issues with the team.

Senior PSLs sometimes move in-house and pursue roles such as director of knowledge at the government legal department. In a similar vein to this role in law firms, they lead the legal knowledge, capacity, and innovation strategy and work with external experts to improve how they create and share legal expertise to streamline and transform the way they deliver legal services to their clients.

Major banks also employ PSLs in roles such as global legal knowledge and training lawyer, which focus on developing in-house knowledge and training within the bank, as well as meeting with the law firms who sit on their legal panel to request training for the lawyers within the bank in the form of specific client training, webinars, or conferences. They may also request that their panel law firms provide free bespoke thought leadership to the bank. Major banks also employ senior PSLs in roles such as head of knowledge, legal.

This demonstrates that not only law firms, but also their own clients, really value the role of PSLs as they employ them as senior in-house lawyers managing their knowhow and training and working within their legal teams.

PSL roles at legal knowledge providers

Some PSLs choose to pursue roles in specific departments within legal knowledge providers such as LexisNexis and Thomson Reuters. At LexisNexis, senior PSLs may be responsible for drafting online guidance on specific areas of law and template documents. They may also develop interactive toolkits and write articles and knowhow materials. In addition, they may act as editors for Lexis PSL's guidance notes and news items. There are also opportunities for PSLs within these legal knowledge providers to become head of departments in which they may focus on delivering market leading content to lawyers as well as focusing on innovative and customer-specific strategies for these departments.

Thomson Reuters hire senior PSLs as senior editors to write content for *Practical Law*, which is a web-based subscription service for lawyers and other business professionals. In this role they may answer subscribers' queries on legal issues, write and edit updates on daily legal developments, write and maintain practice notes, publish content to PLC's website, write content for the monthly bulletin in *PLC Magazine*, and participate in marketing. They will usually support a specific area of law and can also progress into being head of that group.

Consultancy practices

Some very experienced PSLs who have worked in roles such as chief knowledge officer or director of knowledge management have created their own consultancy practices where they provide training and advice on innovation and knowledge sharing systems for the professional services sector. They help law firms become more profitable, innovative, and efficient. They can guide professional service firms and in-house counsel on how to use knowledge, technology, and innovation to improve service delivery and financial performance. They can provide professional service firms and in-house counsel with training and advice/coaching so they can implement their own knowledge systems in a practical and affordable way.

Legal tech

A few PSLs pursue careers in the legal tech industry and join the multitude of legal tech companies in roles such as international strategic growth consultant. However, this career move is a recent development. Legal technology providers would clearly value an experienced lawyer who has previously worked as a senior PSL as they will have the knowledge and experience of an end user of their products and will be well positioned to advise on targeting key legal clients. They will also be able to speak confidently about the legal tech from the perspective of a lawyer and will be able to relate to other senior PSLs and lawyers more easily within the target law firms, which is invaluable as it will help the legal tech company to increase its sales to law firms.

Conclusion

The choice of career paths that PSLs can pursue is diverse and exciting as new opportunities and roles are arising every day in a broad range of sectors, branching out from law firms to industry and businesses as they recognize the essential need to maintain and develop their own internal knowhow and improve efficiency and best practice. The seniority of roles is also appealing with substantial remuneration packages on offer for roles such as global chief knowledge officer. Indeed, lawyers in these roles are going on to create their own consultancy practices, which will be well sought after by law firms and other industries. Lastly, the continued fast-paced emergence of legal tech will certainly create more roles that would be ideally suited to experienced PSLs.

Chapter 3:
The evolution of knowledge management – meeting the future

By Clare Harman Clark, senior professional support lawyer, Taylor Wessing LLP

Introduction

As far as the world is concerned, knowledge is the bread and butter of any law firm. The understanding and application of legal knowledge is at the heart of every single activity undertaken by lawyers; it's what enables us as deal facilitators, as risk assessors, and as future gazers. It's what our clients value and trust. Within their own walls, however, it is still (relatively speaking) early days for the discipline of knowledge management. With three theoretical and academic decades under its belt, KM is now staking out a claim for an extended and specialist professional role within law firms and early professional support lawyer (PSL) pioneers are finding that it demands and develops a uniquely versatile skillset. And so, as increasing numbers of law firms evolve to meet the future, knowledge management is morphing into one of the most challenging, valuable, and exciting roles on offer.

History of KM

Technically speaking, "knowledge management" as a rigorous discipline is a child of the 1990s. A term coined by organizational theorist Ikujiro Nonaka way back in 1991,[1] it stands as collective shorthand for the multidisciplinary strategies involved in creating, sharing, using, and managing an organization's knowledge. As a business strategy, its application was intended to be rolled out across vastly different companies, institutions, and organizations, where it would be as integral to operation as IT or Human Resources departments. By encouraging sharing and innovation, effective knowledge management values knowledge as a central strategic asset and it is credited with ensuring not just a business' continuous improvement, but also its competitive advantage.

Of course, outside the textbooks, the (conscious or unconscious) use of strategies to collate and maximize organizational knowledge have existed far longer. Professional training, associate mentoring, the creation of discussion forums, and the curation of library resources have been commonplace for years in many, many places, not least the law. Indeed, by the early 1990s, many English city firms had introduced the role of professional support lawyer (PSL) in a proto knowledge management function. At the time, the PSL was something akin to a back-office support function. Expectations were set for the role to be filled by a learned black letter expert in the law, someone who could be a specialist sounding-board for fee earner queries, undertake niche research tasks, and draft workable precedents. Now however, as the academic theory in KM gains weight, serious legal organizations are overlaying its teachings to those roles, with the result that by operating as a legal knowledge manager, today's PSL is a very different beast.

Functions of legal KM

Flexibility is key to the role of a legal knowledge manager, together with an almost driving passion for day-to-day diversity. Work in the academic world tends to have general KM strategies revolve around the three suns of organizational capacity, technology, and people interaction, and each one of these components must also be at the heart of any law firm's KM model. In practice, this means that in addition to their own specialist expertise, PSLs are now acquiring considerable new skill sets, ones that often go far beyond legal knowledge and drafting capability.

Bolstering organizational capacity

There must clearly be some rigor to setting a knowledge management strategy and its processes, so that success can be measured, and key lessons learned. From the off, however, framing the motivations behind such a KM strategy is not always simple. The obvious place to start is the demand for broadly improving the efficiency, productivity, and excellence of the law firm itself. This is a fine goal but in many ways the formulation of a strategy to fulfil this is, at this still relatively nascent stage for the discipline, something of a wicked problem. It is a goal with so many incomplete or contradictory strands, with so many changing demands, that it becomes near impossible for one knowledge manager to solve within the confines of a standard working week. It is worthwhile, therefore, breaking down the task into components that will drive the strategy.

Leveraging expertise across an organization involves building the physical and digital architectures to promote knowledge sharing, and key to this is understanding the opportunities for knowledge capture. Quantifiably and qualitatively measuring and reporting on intellectual capital is no mean feat

– not *all* knowledge is actually useful. KM practitioners explain that knowledge may be grabbed at three stages in any exercise – before, during, and after. Both distinct and overlapping, knowledge management techniques might thus variously separate into strategies for black letter law training *before* the associates tackle the deal, template drafting that might be honed *during* a transaction, and deal debriefs for lessons learned *after* the event.

When it comes to how that knowledge is shared, the academics talk about a push and pull approach. It is probably fair to say that firms with established PSLs are used to a push structure, whereby the PSL looks explicitly to push their own technical knowledge and expertise onto a shared knowledge repository. They proactively take on responsibility for keeping up to date with and understanding as much of the law as possible. They manage the knowledge database and proactively collate specific knowledge that others might have produced. In the alternative, a pull strategy is much more proactive about approaching individual experts across an organization and asking for ad hoc input. Knowledge brokers might be appointed across a firm or practice area to take on responsibility for specific or niche areas, and act as a first port of call when questions arise.

Whether pushing or pulling, knowledge managers should map competencies and experiences across the practice and try new ways of fostering the sharing of learning. It is almost inevitable that intellectual capital in a law firm is highly personalized, with specific knowledge possessed by certain individuals or teams. Most law firms operate on the basis that people will just *know* who to ask. They *know* because they *know* someone who's asked before. Every day names are proffered and experts recommended based on previous personal experiences; such flexing professional networks are alive and well but almost entirely unwritten. Against this, mapping specialisms formally (and in granular detail) makes it easier to identify gaps.

This exercise also helps to avoid the loss of knowledge when lawyers leave a firm, dismantling barriers to retaining knowledge in a meaningful sense and bolstering the resilience of that overall intellectual capital. This should be a process less about facilitating periodic brain dumps and more about qualitatively assessing knowledge in terms of its often time-limited complexity and usefulness. The academic jury is still out on the effectiveness of the incentivization carrot when it comes to asking nicely for fee earner engagement in knowledge collation workstreams, but by embedding performance targets into the general appraisal system (i.e., using more of a stick), firms can require continual work on knowledge competencies or sharing. Redrafting appraisal goals requires some overarching management buy-in for the KM strategy, but associates can then be expected routinely to conduct deal debriefs, add templates to repositories, draft articles, or even mentor juniors. Knowledge is valued as central to the operation.

Excitingly for practitioners, leveraging legal knowledge expertise now involves workstreams both within and outside the law firm. In recent years, the internal operational brief has expanded to put the legal knowledge manager in a considerably more outward facing role. Many are already actively engaged in the production of outward-facing thought leadership, published for the market or specific clients. Many also offer client support and training that extends far beyond the completion of a transaction. Done well, the knowledge manager has a key role therefore in embedding the law firm into a stickier (and more productive) client relationship.

As relationships outside the firm deepen, there is also scope to engage in one of the most challenging tasks of knowledge management: capturing and utilizing *interorganizational* knowledge. Now perhaps more than ever there is scope not just to teach clients, to impart knowledge to them, but also to learn from them, and bring those findings back to the law firm. Putting knowledge management at the heart of any supply chain relationship is challenging – no more so when individual companies manage and share differently, and when lawyer-client relationships are routinely characterized by confidentiality – but in some of the largest issues facing us today as lawyers and as people, there is tremendous potential in approaching knowledge as a continual two-way street.

Consider the climate emergency, for example. Practically speaking, not only is it rare to find a lawyer who moonlights as a climate scientist, but also there is not yet any real market standard for legal drafting that deals with environmental, social, and governmental (ESG) issues in many practice areas. For a law firm to recommend importing sustainability provisions into its client's real estate, financing, or corporate deals for example, it needs first to collect knowledge from the client, the market, and peers. It must build networks with relevant specialist individuals. The Digital Revolution has dramatically increased the accessibility of knowledge, but the sheer quantity, speed, and complexity of this requires a dialectic filter.

Bridging the technology gap

The second strand to the knowledge management bow is technological. In many cases, PSLs have been at the heart of inward-facing practice management development for many years, both creating and curating a practice area's knowledge. However, the workstream that started originally as the drafting and lever-arch-filing of new transaction precedents, or the creation of static transaction checklists, has changed. It turned first into assisting IT with the development of slightly more technological knowledge storage solutions (and understanding database taxonomies). Now it encompasses the identification and implementation of a wide range of tech tools and processes to drive efficiencies across the whole practice.

Every modern law firm needs at least a searchable repository for its vast swathes of accumulated information and data-led assistance for its decision-making. There are countless off the shelf database options ready to oblige. But moving beyond this, whether by exploring the holy grail tech tool of accurate fee quotation, on-boarding visualization products to assist with early deal diligence, or automating those Word precedents for one-click document production, knowledge managers are key to selecting and efficiently harnessing all sorts of products from the available legal tech.

This is often a complicated process as many of the tools on offer have overlapping functionality, but broadly they may offer collaborative software technologies (such as the threaded discussions on Microsoft Teams or knowledge sharing on wiki forums), eLearning tools, content/document management systems, workflow systems, or even AI products to extract and interpret data from commoditized contracts, as part of a due diligence exercise. The selection and analysis of these lie far outside the traditional remit of a PSL, so that today's knowledge managers are using a skill set that goes a long way beyond researching, categorizing, and explaining the law.

Indeed, as the burgeoning market delivers ever more tech options, the role of knowledge manager is in many cases that of quasi product designer. Many of these tools do not even relate to KM tech in the traditional sense of that digital knowledge database; nonetheless practitioners are developing rigorous structures to choose between products, capture opportunities, and drive efficiencies. It could even mean working closely with the software developer to address a particular problem or practice inefficiency. By understanding both the law and the deal, knowledge managers are uniquely placed to bridge the gap between software potential and practice area need.

Encouraging and empowering people

Last but by no means least, a law firm is nothing without its quality lawyers, and PSLs have long been tasked with structuring the professional development of this intellectual capital, both collating and then sharing knowledge between working teams. As offices develop flexible working strategies, however, the focus on people is ever more important and KM professionals must be a step ahead in understanding how to harness and promote the sharing of information and best practice.

On an academic level, there are different frameworks for categorizing different types of knowledge. Leaning back on Nonaka,[2] we might distinguish between tacit (internalized) and explicit (conscious) knowledge, for example, and the strategies for banking and communicating each type is different. This situation is further complicated by the fast-moving change in our post-pandemic world. As associates adopt different working schedules, for example, we must explore moving beyond whole group in-person training sessions, a traditionally explicit and somewhat didactic tool to share knowledge. New eLearning software packages can help by using story telling or action-oriented training to unlock some of the tacit knowledge that might have seemed otherwise out of reach.

Similarly, we can no longer rely on water cooler conversations to catch up on more tacit news and views. Such interactions are the traditional office lifeblood of team cohesion and a central way of picking up (often unconsciously) on the kind of contextual knowledge that is crucial to a practice area's operations. They routinely revolve around topics that are often harder to explain in a formal training session. Understanding these (and other) "communities of practice" that keep a department running might mean the knowledge manager is working to influence behaviors or embed cultural shifts that are difficult in the fast-moving, disjointed, and time-poor world in which success has traditionally meant keeping clients and transactions close.

Knowing the future

This is an exciting time to be in knowledge management in a law firm. There are certainly challenges, not least in putting your arms effectively around the shifting job description, but legal knowledge experts are carving a vital, dynamic, and exhilarating space within the future law firm. They are central to the creation and curation of legal knowledge, to driving the adoption of new legal tech tools, and they are looking firmly to the future of a practice's team cohesion, talent development, and working efficiency. They are following in the traditional footsteps of the PSL but wearing far larger boots. And making some giant leaps for their law firms as they go.

References

1. "The knowledge creating company", *Harvard Business Review*. 69 (6): pp. 96-104. https://memberfiles.freewebs.com/84/90/65819084/documents/The%20Knowledge-Creating%20Company.pdf
2. *Ibid.*

Chapter 4:
Pro bono management

By Amy Grunske, head of international pro bono, sustainability and community responsibility, Orrick

The last two plus decades have seen an exponential growth in the number of full-time roles dedicated to pro bono management as law firms recognize that in order to maximize their societal impact and gain the full benefits of their pro bono practices, they need a dedicated professional to lead them.

What is pro bono?

Within the legal sector the term pro bono is defined slightly differently across jurisdictions. In its simplest form, pro bono refers to the provision of legal services by qualified lawyers (or in some instances, individuals training to be lawyers, such as those in "graduate" or "trainee" roles) at no cost, for the social good.

It is typical for definitions to include qualification around type of beneficiaries, focusing on individuals of limited means or otherwise inadequate access to legal assistance, and non-profit organizations that are unable to pay for legal services of reasonable cost. In some definitions, limited work for social enterprises, government, and educational organizations is also included. In general, global and large national firms in the jurisdictions of the US, UK, and Australia tend to follow the definitions of pro bono organizations such as the Pro Bono Institute, the Australian Pro Bono Centre, and TrustLaw.

How many dedicated pro bono roles are available?

The Association of Pro Bono Counsel (APBCo) is the only global membership organization for full-time professionals who manage law firm pro bono practices. As of January 2022, it has 290 members across 13 countries and from 130 law firms.[1] Although the majority of these members are located within the US, a jurisdiction with the longest history of professionalized pro bono roles, 20 percent of APBCo members now reside and work in other jurisdictions. In the UK specifically, the most recent survey (released in January 2022) by the national pro bono membership organization, the UK Collaborative Plan for Pro Bono, found that there are 65 pro bono professionals employed across 43 member firms.[2] In Australia, the latest Australian Pro Bono Centre National Law Firm Pro Bono Survey for firms larger than 50 lawyers (released in February 2021) reported that 29 firms had at least one full-time pro bono professional.[3] There are currently limited numbers of additional dedicated pro bono professionals in other jurisdictions, for example South Africa, France, Germany, and China. As more global firms recognize the importance of locally led pro bono programs, and national firms in other jurisdictions understand the importance of dedicated roles in this space, these numbers will no doubt increase significantly.

"In the 1970s, provoked by the poverty law movement and the broader civil rights movement, America's largest law firms began to set up pro bono programs focused on meeting the legal needs of low-income communities. In the 1980s and 1990s as civil legal aid funding was decimated, those same firms began to professionalize their pro bono programs to meet the need. They adopted pro bono policies, established pro bono committees, and appointed full-time pro bono managers. Today, you will find full-time pro bono managers, and sometimes even entire departments, mandated to run law firm pro bono programs at each and every one of the top 100 or so US law firms.

"The decade between 1990 and 2000 saw unprecedented economic growth and an explosion in international commerce. This was also the period during which the world's largest law firms – mainly US firms but also some London firms made up of hundreds of thousands of lawyers – rapidly internationalized, opening offices across the globe. As they expanded around the globe, they took their pro bono cultures with them. In the words of Suzie Turner (partner and chair of Dechert's firm-wide pro bono practice, talking in 2003), 'our commitment to pro bono is global in nature…one firm, one commitment, one policy'. Talking in 2015, she put it another way: 'There is legal need in all jurisdictions, so to require pro bono in the US but not in Kazakhstan does not hold water'.[4]

"This gave rise to the prospect of the global institutionalization of pro bono, something that is in fact coming to fruition in places like the United Kingdom, Australia, Continental Europe, and although more slowly, outside of the global West in countries such as Brazil, Singapore and India. Through global behemoths such as Baker & Makenzie, DLA Piper, and Dentons and global referral networks such as TrustLaw, today we can truly speak of the globalized practice

of pro bono. Barely a corner of the world remains untouched by the footprint of commercial law firm pro bono programming.

"To ensure firms are genuinely addressing legal need in all parts of the world through their growing pro bono practice, and remain responsive to the local legal, social, and political context, they are slowly recognizing the importance of creating dedicated pro bono roles based in these different regions and jurisdictions. Local champions, native to the relevant national legal system, are essential to the long term viability of pro bono."
Lamin Khadar, sustainability and pro bono lawyer, Dentons

What responsibilities are included in the role?

The responsibilities of pro bono professionals can differ depending on jurisdiction, size of the firm and pro bono team, and firm culture. In some firms, pro bono professionals are responsible for a wider Corporate Social Responsibility (CSR) or Environmental, Social, and Governance (ESG) program, coordinating other aspects of responsible business such as non-legal volunteering, charitable giving, and sustainability.

"Integrating the pro bono and community service roles allows our team to see our firm as a whole and find ways for every member of our professional staff to find ways to make an impact and give back to their communities. This can lead to powerful synergies."
Elizabeth Lewis, pro bono and community service partner, McDermott Will & Emery

"At Charles Russell Speechlys, our pro bono practice is an important part of our wider Responsible Business Program. That program encompasses – and helps us to coordinate – all of the work we do to integrate, understand, and improve our environmental and social impact as a business and the work we do to support our clients to do the same."
Kerry Stares, partner, responsible business and pro bono, Charles Russell Speechlys

In other firms, these roles are distinct.

"From the start, my role was as a lawyer leading the firm's pro bono practice and running pro bono cases, as distinct from any 'community' or 'corporate social responsibility' parts of the firm. This focused role helped to 'mainstream' our pro bono practice, and integrate it fully within the firm. It gave my work, and pro

bono work more generally, credibility as 'real' legal work, emphasized pro bono clients as clients of the firm, gave me and my pro bono team credibility as 'real lawyers' with specialist skills who are on a career track, and supported a deliberate policy that pro bono work was expected to be a fundamental part of every lawyer's legal practice. This strategy has worked well, both for the career paths of our specialist pro bono lawyers and for our firm participation in pro bono in general – we have one of Australia's largest dedicated pro bono teams, including two partners and two senior associates, and very high (more than 90 percent) pro bono participation rates by partners and lawyers throughout the firm."
David Hillard, pro bono partner, Clayton Utz

"At my firm the pro bono practice is managed separately from our CSR/community service efforts, although of course there is tremendous overlap with those areas. Just focusing on pro bono has given me the necessary capacity to develop and manage a large practice that includes all of our offices across the globe and incorporates all our practice groups, enabling our lawyers to use their talent, passion, and creativity to tackle important issues and help bridge the justice gap."
Katie Marquart, partner and pro bono chair, Gibson Dunn

Either way, the large majority of pro bono professionals are qualified lawyers, reflecting the reality that law firm pro bono work requires the same level of oversight as any other legal practice.

Some pro bono professionals also maintain an active caseload in a particular area of public interest specialization, alongside their coordination and leadership responsibilities. This can be advantageous in terms of increasing knowledge and expertise in the areas the firm is focusing their pro bono work on, and being able to supervise the work in-house rather than solely relying on guidance and training from specialist lawyers that are employed at partner legal services organizations, law centers, and legal non-governmental organizations (NGOs).

"Our pro bono lawyers are encouraged to devote a proportion of their time to legal work on pro bono matters. I think this is helpful to our standing within the firm and within the wider advice sector. It also ensures we stay up-to-date in particular areas of law in which we provide technical assistance and supervision within the firm."
Paul Yates, counsel, head of pro bono, Freshfields

"I believe it is critical that the pro bono professional have substantive expertise to lead the practice so that lawyers have an internal resource for their pro

bono work. This also facilitates greater depth of knowledge that allows firms to develop expertise to work on difficult and impactful pro bono matters independent of resource constrained legal services partner organizations."
Rene Kathawala, pro bono counsel, Orrick

However, the ability to maintain an active caseload as well as management can be difficult and is dependent on capacity, taking into consideration factors such as the size of the firm, the size of the pro bono team, and how developed the firm's pro bono practice is.

"Over my 20 plus years as a pro bono professional I have covered all aspects of setting up and running a pro bono program (the largest/small firm, domestic/ international, civil/common law, private practice/NGO, casework/management). I now concentrate solely on management but without doubt the ten years I spent practicing enable me to do the role as currently structured, in particular evaluating and scoping opportunities, risk management, and a real understanding of our volunteer lawyers. Without running a caseload I can leverage my time more effectively in terms of developing the practice and engaging more lawyers. With the time I would spend handling one matter, I can source 20 matters involving 40 plus lawyers, in line with the firm's objectives."
Felicity Kirk, international pro bono, Ropes & Gray

What are the usual job titles for dedicated pro bono roles?

The title and level of internal seniority of pro bono professionals can vary significantly across firms depending on jurisdiction, size of the firm and the pro bono team, and firm culture. Given the complexities of pro bono legal work it is typical for at least one of the dedicated pro bono roles at a firm to be a senior legal role such as partner or counsel, or a senior business services role such as director of pro bono or head of pro bono. Other titles can include:

- Pro bono specialist;
- Special counsel for pro bono;
- Pro bono lawyer;
- Pro bono attorney;
- Pro bono manager;
- Pro bono legal officer; and
- Pro bono coordinator.

Some bigger pro bono teams may also have pro bono professionals that focus on managing pro bono in a particular area of law, for example:

- Pro bono immigration attorney;
- Senior pro bono trial attorney;
- Pro bono managing attorney for tax-exempt organizations;
- Pro bono counsel for racial justice initiatives; and
- Pro bono associate for corporate, impact investment and charities law.

There has been a positive trend of firms acknowledging the importance of a dedicated partner role over the past decade, with a significant increase in the numbers of positions available in the US, Australia, and more recently the UK.

> *"The nature of pro bono work has evolved enormously over the last decade. Pro bono practices are much larger and often operate across multiple jurisdictions. The work is increasingly complex, frequently connected to humanitarian emergencies, and almost always requires strategic engagement with a range of stakeholders. The growth in pro bono partner roles directly reflects these trends."*[5]
> **Nic Patrick**, partner, pro bono and responsible business, DLA Piper

> *"Commercial firms are now recognizing that leadership in pro bono at a partner level is necessary to provide an effective practice. This is also important if law firms are to continue to be seen as an integral part of the justice system and to demonstrate their wider contribution to society. The path to partnership is always about demonstrating the contribution to the firm, and it is no different for pro bono lawyers. The investment by firms in their pro bono practices is incredibly valuable and needs to be well directed to the specialist knowledge and expertise of an experienced pro bono professional. This is the only way to achieve a genuine impact and be able to harness the true potential of the firm to address some of the most intractable inequities across the world."*
> **Yasmin Waljee OBE**, partner, international pro bono, Hogan Lovells

What skills do I need to be a pro bono professional?

The development and ongoing management of a high-quality pro bono practice is complex, requires a broad set of diverse skills, and takes a significant amount of time and effort. Successful pro bono professionals require:

- Strong leadership skills to build and maintain a culture of pro bono at their firm. They need the interpersonal and communication expertise to inspire, empower, and even at times persuade colleagues at their firms to get involved in pro bono work on top of their busy billable practices. Not only that, they need to develop and encourage participation in matters and projects that may not necessarily be aligned with that particular individual's interest and passion, but address the greatest unmet legal need, and structured such that it is the most efficient and effective use of legal skills and maximizing overall impact.
- A basis of generalist legal knowledge and an ability to quickly understand different areas of both transactional and litigation-based law such that they can properly consider unmet legal needs and have the necessary scoping conversations with potential clients and project partners for new matters and initiatives.
- The ability to be big picture strategic thinkers, comfortable with leading high-level discussions with firm management about the direction of the practice, drafting and seeking approval on annual and longer-term strategic plans, and obtaining the necessary top-down visible support for the expansion and direction of the practice. They also need to understand the role of pro bono within the business structure, and be fully cognizant of and able to capture the strategic benefits of pro bono to the firm as a profit-making organization. Pro bono can be an important tool in developing and maintaining commercial client relationships, as an important element of responses to tender requests and in client pitches, as well as providing a unique opportunity to partner with in-house legal teams of corporate clients. Pro bono can also be an integral part of an effective recruitment and retention strategy for a firm. This is particularly the case for the younger generation of lawyers who not only appreciate but expect their firm to provide them with opportunities to use their legal skills for the benefit of society, and can also obtain significant training benefit from the additional skills and responsibility that pro bono matters can offer.
- Written communication skills necessary to draft effective internal and external publication materials promoting the program. They need to be skilled in business development, fostering networks, and building relationships with non-profit organizations, and generating pipelines of work that they will then assess and approve before allocating to

appropriate colleagues. They need to be adept at building networks within their firms, not only with fee earning legal colleagues but also with business units such as the HR, marketing, and finance teams.

- A deep understanding of the importance of proper risk assessment and management, including potential conflicts of interest, and the ability to recognize and implement best practice for matter placement, active supervision, and proper file management to ensure all work is consistent with regulations and standards. Pro bono professionals will manage an operational budget that will include program costs and disbursements and must work closely with the firm's finance teams and billing systems to monitor and ensure appropriate resources are being spent on the pro bono practice. Data management and evaluation expertise is also needed to undertake periodic reporting on appropriate metrics and make meaningful assessments against strategic aims.

"My primary focus in my role is to develop collaborations with non-profit organizations that provide pro bono legal services and access to justice to individuals and organizations who cannot afford or secure specialized legal expertise. I also work to promote pro bono engagement internally amongst fee-earners. Developing specialized pro bono casework with colleagues in the sector involves identifying an unmet legal need or a pressing issue where pro bono recourses can have a meaningful impact. This typically starts with building a relationship with an expert organization, and then working through the logistics to make the project a reality. This can involve having conversations with project NGO partners and the firm's leadership, drafting legal documents, as well as engaging with colleagues across departments, from risk management to marketing. Once a project is finally off the ground, my primary role is to serve as a resource to the firm's lawyers when they engage in pro bono work. I also provide guidance and supervision on pro bono casework in areas where I have developed expertise."
Marika Somero, pro bono manager, solicitor, Debevoise & Plimpton

"I love the variety in this job, you get the chance to do a bit of everything – people management, strategy planning, legal casework, public speaking, risk analysis, marketing, and setting up impactful projects to help individuals access justice. The best part of the role is the people we work with, our enthusiastic lawyers who want to help others, our amazing NGO partners that go above and beyond to assist vulnerable people, and our clients whose resilience and hope keeps us working hard on cases every day."
Becca Naylor, senior associate, head of pro bono EMEA, Reed Smith

"Being both a global practice head for pro bono and a global function head for social impact, I have enormous amount of variety in the work that I do, especially working across so many countries and offices. My role is often akin to being a CEO of a not-for-profit law firm, where I focus on strategy, resource allocation for maximum impact, talent, culture, and the creation of shared value. Often I become more of a traditional legal partner who gives direct legal advice to clients, usually individuals who are experiencing marginalization and disadvantage. I also play a broader role of ESG advisor, both internally and externally, and am considered an expert particularly with regard to the 'social' aspects of ESG."
Sarah Morton-Ramwell, partner, global head of pro bono and social impact, Ashurst

What is a typical day like in a pro bono role?

Given how broad the usual responsibilities of these roles are as described above, there is usually no "typical" day for a pro bono professional.

"There's no 'typical' day for a pro bono professional, and that's what I love about it. My role, and thus any one of my days, falls into three buckets – internal practice management, external engagement, and client representation. Each bucket can overlap with another, but each presents different challenges and opportunities. As a practice manager, I might be interacting with Akin Gump colleagues in Hong Kong, London, or Los Angeles on a given day. The interaction may be a brief email, a longer phone call, or a more formal meeting. Externally, I engage with legal services organizations, my colleagues at other firms, the media, law students, and commercial clients about pro bono generally or specific projects. My favorite part of the role – and one I will never surrender – is working directly with clients, particularly asylum seekers. So on a given day you might find me in immigration court, an asylum office, or counseling a client seeking refuge."
Steve Schulman, pro bono partner, Akin Gump

"My days are full and varied, which keeps the job interesting and engaging. In a firm of our size and global footprint, there is a constant flow of questions to be resolved. I am based in New York but with most of our offices outside the United States, I wake up every morning to several dozen emails that have come in overnight from around the world. I spend a good deal of time on risk management for the firm – helping vet potential pro bono matters with partners and our global pro bono practice leader and head of global citizenship to ensure that they are appropriate, conflict free, and fit within our policies. On

any given day, I might also have a call with a new NGO or referral organization to discuss possible collaboration, join in mooting an associate about to argue a pro bono criminal appeal in court, coordinate with our internal communications team to propose a story on a recent win, help manage a major global research project, review case lists that have come in, comment on an engagement letter, and of course collaborate throughout the day with our small but incredibly dedicated pro bono team."
Lou O'Neil, global pro bono counsel, White & Case

"I often begin with a catch up meeting – with our pro bono team, reporting on work underway or with our community engagement team, discussing what needs attention with our philanthropy, sustainability, and reconciliation programs. After that, there's little pattern to the days – more a kind of controlled chaos as I endeavor to respond to urgent needs, make headway on ongoing projects, and look after people. Many days include troubleshooting – usually working through a risk issue that's arisen on a matter: we might discover a conflict we didn't initially know about or I might be alerted to challenges working with a client experiencing trauma. In short, I manage and I mentor and I market, I advise and I strategize – usually before lunch. I learn something new every day, identify something I could have done better every day and, on a good day, relish something that went well."
Nicky Friedman, director of community engagement, Allens

"The primary goal of a pro bono counsel is to connect need in our communities to the interests and resources within our firms, and then to build and manage the infrastructure required to deliver the firm's assistance in a safe and responsible way. That means every day is different. Any given Monday could include meeting with a public interest colleague to develop a new clinic, interviewing a client, training lawyers on a new skillset, problem-solving with a legal team, collaborating across firms on an international project, or celebrating a success with a lawyer who has made a difference in a client's life. Time spent at work ranges from understanding potential conflicts involved in a representation to seeing someone walk out of a courthouse with newly secured freedom. One thing holds true every day – there is a great sense of purpose and responsibility that carries through each moment."
Brenna DeVaney, director of pro bono programs and pro bono counsel, Skadden, Arps, Slate, Meagher & Flom

"A typical day could start with a call to a pro bono professional at another firm to discuss ideas for progressing a new pro bono initiative that several firms

are involved in. After that I switch to focusing on modern slavery, thinking through how to engage different legal departments, what training is required and which organizations we could approach to discuss pro bono support. That's followed by a meeting with our apprentice who I'm training on the different types of submissions that organizations make to international human rights mechanisms, as we are often asked to assist with these. With training over, I finalize the team of lawyers who will assist with a new project and ensure the briefing session with the lead organization is in the diary. Final task of the day: checking in with a couple of our global offices about new matters they are hoping to take on."

Rebecca Greenhalgh, counsel, pro bono, Ashurst

"Here at Husch, I spearhead the firm's pro bono initiative dedicated to representing minority businesses, as a means of helping them create jobs for other minorities and to expand wealth, equity, and opportunity to all. Each day is exciting and different. Generally, I spend some of the day talking with minority entrepreneurs about their businesses, discussing the growth of their companies. Usually, I can sense the excitement in their voices. Sometimes, I sense frustration and fatigue. And my heart goes out. Raising a business is not for the faint-hearted or the 'corner-cutters'. Also, I spend the day reading applications to our program, welcoming new applicants with a telephone call, making decisions about which companies are ready for representation and which are not. Finally, many days I have the chance to directly help companies by guest-speaking at training events. I love the variety of my job and the potential to be of service to so many."

Quinncy McNeal, pro bono counsel, Husch Blackwell

What support is available for pro bono professionals?

A number of global, regional, and local organizations have been created to provide assistance with pro bono management at law firms and support to pro bono professionals in their work and the development of their careers. These organizations facilitate discussions on important topics such as risk management, monitoring and evaluation, and the most effective and efficient models of pro bono assistance, as well as help professionals connect with and learn from each other, and collaborate on projects and causes.

More information on just some of the many organizations, from the perspective of pro bono professionals, are below.

"APBCo is the only global pro bono professional membership organization, made up of over 290 attorneys and practice group managers who run pro bono practices in over 130 of the world's largest law firms. It was created by and is run

by pro bono professionals, for pro bono professionals. I, alongside so many of my colleagues, have benefited greatly from the support of the organization over the last 15 years. APBCo facilitates the creation of comprehensive materials on professional development and challenges relating to pro bono management, runs an annual conference and ad hoc programming sessions throughout the year, and also hosts Chatter, a messaging system where all members can connect easily and quickly with one another to ask any questions on particular issues they are experiencing and work together on projects and matters."
Tiffany Graves, pro bono counsel, Bradley Arant Boult Cummings, on behalf of the APBCo Board

"Throughout my career I have benefited from the work of PBI and the support they provide to pro bono professionals. Their comprehensive definition of pro bono and related guidance form the basis of many large firm pro bono practices, articulating a single standard that emphasizes the legal needs of low income, underserved groups while also contemplating a range of work to advance human rights, civil rights, and public rights. PBI also organizes a conference in the US each year for law firm pro bono professionals, legal aid lawyers, and in-house legal counsel who are involved in running pro bono programs at their organizations. The conference provides a great opportunity for in-depth discussion around pro bono topics, as well as the chance to build important connections between those working in this space."
Wendy Atrokhov, public service counsel, director of global pro bono, Latham & Watkins, on behalf of Pro Bono Institute

"When I transitioned from the commercial legal sector to the pro bono sector in 2014, I had no clue how to build and run a pro bono practice in a large commercial law firm. I was however very quickly welcomed into the pro bono sector by John Corker, the then CEO of Australian Pro Bono Centre, and introduced to the broader pro bono network and the wealth of resources made available by the Centre, including practical resources, guides, and programs to help create and maintain a pro bono program. In 2017 I became a director of the Centre and in recent years, under new CEO Gabriela Christian-Hare, have seen the strategic focus of the Centre and the resources made available by the Centre grow from strength to strength. Having recently been appointed as the new head of pro bono at HopgoodGanim Lawyers, and tasked with building the firm's pro bono practice, I will again look to the Centre's resources for best practice guidance."
Leanne Collingburn, head of pro bono, HopgoodGanim, on behalf of Australian Pro Bono Centre

"The UK Collaborative Plan (UKCP) is a profession-led initiative for law firms set up in 2014. This free network has been invaluable in bringing law firms together to grow their pro bono practices. Member firms work collaboratively to develop the systems and infrastructure to allow pro bono services to be effectively delivered to address unmet legal need. The group meets quarterly and participates in an active email listserv where we refer matters to each other, find other firms to work with on projects, and discuss topical issues. Member firms share pro bono data anonymously and commit to an aspirational target of an average of 25 hours of pro bono work per lawyer. UKCP also facilitates regular programming throughout the year on topics such as access to justice, and UKademy, the full day professional development conference for UKCP members, which is now an annual event."
Marion Edge, pro bono counsel, Dechert, on behalf of the Collaborative Plan for Pro Bono Secretariat

"The European Pro Bono Initiative was set up in 2019 by pro bono managers working for international law firms managing their firm's pro bono practices in Continental Europe. It has been such a helpful resource to me and my colleagues to help us connect with each other and share best practices, resources, and ideas to increase pro bono engagement at our firms. We also work together to research barriers to access to justice in Europe for vulnerable individuals and identify growth opportunities for pro bono in the region."
Özgür Kahale, director of pro bono for Europe, DLA Piper, on behalf of the Steering Committee of the European Pro Bono Initiative

"PILnet is a global NGO that focuses on unlocking the potential of pro bono, encouraging and facilitating free legal assistance to civil society organizations around the world in partnership with major multinational and local and regional law firms and independent practitioners. Many pro bono professionals, including myself, work closely with the PILnet team and greatly benefit from the resources and support they provide. PILnet runs several pro bono clearinghouses that match NGO legal needs with qualified pro bono lawyers and works with both sides to create a strategic partnership for sustained impact. PILnet also runs the biggest event in the world dedicated to pro bono – the Global Pro Bono Forum. The Forum is organized annually and convenes over 400 representatives from the private legal sector and NGO sector from around the world to connect and collaborate with each other, discuss new ideas for pro bono projects, and develop innovative strategies for using the law to protect civil society."
Atanas Politov, Europe director of pro bono, Dentons, on behalf of PILnet

"TrustLaw is the Thomson Reuters Foundation's global pro bono legal program which provides a fantastic (and free!) resource for pro bono professionals that I and so many of my colleagues have benefited from over the years. Their weekly clearinghouse email sets out a detailed list of interesting and varied pro bono projects from charities, non-profits, and social enterprises from all over the world needing a range of legal advice, from help drafting an employment contract to detailed legal research on a particular human rights subject. They also provide very helpful resources and guides including their TrustLaw Index of pro bono, a widely used benchmark on pro bono participation in different jurisdictions which includes a comprehensive definition of what should count as pro bono and what shouldn't – a tool that encourages and facilitates the spread of the practice of pro bono across the globe."
Sarah Farrelly, pro bono associate, Charles Russell Speechlys, on behalf of TrustLaw

How do I become a pro bono professional?

Those that are interested in a dedicated pro bono role in a law firm may be reassured to learn that there is no clear path to being a pro bono professional, in any jurisdiction.

In many firms the drive to create a pro bono role or team has come from firm management; however, in some cases passionate lawyers have successfully submitted a business case to their firm proposing the establishment of a dedicated role.

A significant number of pro bono professionals have come from a billable background and had been heavily involved in pro bono work before making the move to a dedicated role either at their firm or another. A smaller number of pro bono professionals come from a university background or a public interest law background, having worked in the legal aid or NGO sector, and/or public policy. Some pro bono professionals worked in pro bono clearinghouses or other pro bono organizations before moving to firms.

It must also be noted that as the profession grows there is an increasing awareness and recognition of the importance of diversity within these dedicated roles and a shared commitment to employ more lawyers from the communities that these roles seek to serve.[6]

"My path to pro bono partner was a winding journey. I attended law school to be a civil legal aid lawyer, and I started my career at Legal Aid Chicago. I didn't foresee leaving, but life intervened with our first child. I decided to try BigLaw, with the intention to stay one year. Seven years later, I was an equity partner.

But I grew weary of private practice and the Illinois Attorney General hired me as public interest division chief. It was fantastic to be a public interest lawyer with subpoena power. Five years later, I received a call from a friend, inviting me to apply for pro bono partner at Dentons. 'What is that?' I responded. It turns out that having been a legal aid lawyer, an associate/partner at a large law firm, and on the AG's senior staff was very good preparation for being pro bono partner."
Ben Weinberg, pro bono Partner, Dentons

"My career before moving to pro bono included almost ten years in public service as a public defender and civil rights attorney, two years as an associate at a corporate law firm, and one year as a judicial clerk. This varied experience in the public sector, including criminal and civil litigation and policy work, as well as my experience at a corporate law firm, really prepared me well to manage the broad array of systemic racial justice initiatives that I now lead on in my current role. The step into the pro bono world has been a great one – I feel grateful to have the opportunity to work with a firm with a stated commitment to racial justice pro bono, and to leverage pro bono resources to support the work of community-based organizations, non-profits, and advocates actively committed to undoing systemic racism and injustice."
Diane Lucas, pro bono counsel for racial justice initiatives, David Polk

"I began my career with a top tier commercial law firm and practiced for a number of years there following qualification. Alongside my day job I volunteered weekly with a law center. I saw first-hand the gap between access and the need for legal services by people in the community. In 2011 my career path changed quite dramatically and brought me to South Africa, Tanzania, and Malawi where I developed and implemented a wide variety of rule of law projects. In 2013 I returned to Ireland and began working with the Public Interest Law Alliance (PILA). While at PILA I worked with NGO and law firm colleagues to scope and design impactful pro bono projects. This experience really stood to me when I joined A&L Goodbody to lead the firm's pro bono practice in 2018. Since then, we've expanded considerably our human rights work and I am incredibly proud of the contributions made by so many of my colleagues to tackle the most systemic problems facing our society."
Eithne Lynch, pro bono associate, A&L Goodbody

"I was a year into my role as a commercial real estate solicitor when I handed my notice in; I knew that fee earning was not for me. I wanted to combine my legal skills with project management and social impact. Pro bono management

was just that, but I lived and worked in Birmingham and the vast majority of pro bono roles were London-based for City firms. I made the move south, started applying for roles and asked anyone who would listen for tips on breaking into pro bono management as an external candidate. One of those conversations led to a nine-month contract lawyer role with pro bono broker and charity TrustLaw, and next a three-month policy internship with fellow broker Advocates for International Development. When Linklaters advertised a pro bono legal officer role in 2016, I'd combined my commercial CV with a year of experience in the broker side of the sector."
Sophie Brambley, managing associate (pro bono), Linklaters

"Like many law students, I sought work in the public interest space early on, including with a women's rights organization in India, the Legal Aid Board in South Africa, and supporting program management for women offenders within the national probation service in London. When I started my training contract at a commercial firm in London, I continued building on this experience through the firm's pro bono program. I balanced pro bono commitments with a fee earning practice and increasingly gained an insight into the management and strategy side – how areas of need were identified, building relationships with potential partner organizations and project design, in the context of commercial law firm pro bono. I championed the take up of opportunities within my team and launched a project within the firm. When the opportunity for my current role at A&O came up, it was an obvious move at the right time."
Aditi Kapoor, pro bono manager, Allen & Overy

"My career has exclusively been in the social justice sector, ranging from community legal center work to the Attorney General's Department to now being with Ashurst. In each role I've held, I have been the first or first and only Aboriginal lawyer in the position – there remain many barriers for First Nations Peoples in Australia and it is an honor to serve the community through my role, but it also speaks to the dire need of recognition through lived experience as expertise. As I have observed, my law degree and the wider legal profession possess many limitations due to lack of cultural understanding. What drives my role is the unique lived experience I hold. It is important for those looking to get into pro bono to assess how they can bring their lived experience to shape and legitimize the role. Don't be afraid to break the mold!"
Trent Wallace, First Nations lead, pro bono, Ashurst

"Having completed a commercial training contract, I wanted to stay within the legal sector, but pursue a career within social responsibility. As I was coming

to the end of my training contract, a six-month role became available within the firm's pro bono team, which ticked all the boxes for me. I completed the six-month contract, and then stayed on as a permanent pro bono associate for over four years. In 2018 I moved to Baker McKenzie to manage their pro bono practice and have been there ever since. To anyone interested in a pro bono career, I would recommend connecting with a range of pro bono professionals and getting involved in as much pro bono work as possible, to give you the best possible chance of success when roles come up!"
Stas Kuzmierkiewicz, senior pro bono associate, Baker McKenzie

The pro bono professional role is challenging, varied, far-reaching, and incredibly rewarding. It can be a wonderful career step for a lawyer of any background with a passion for social justice, and the sector welcomes and encourages those who are interested to join us in our work.

References

1. https://apbco.org/
2. http://probonoplan.uk/wp-content/uploads/2022/02/UKCP-20-21-Infographic.pdf
3. www.probonocentre.org.au/wp-content/uploads/2021/02/Survey-Report-FINAL.pdf
4. www.pilnet.org/wp-content/uploads/2020/03/Pro_Bono_Final_Report_V2-1.pdf
5. For further discussion on this topic see www.dlapiper.com/en/us/news/2020/02/new-report-reveals-a-significant-increase-in-pro-bono-partners/.
6. For further discussion on diversity within the pro bono profession see www.dlapiper.com/en/australia/insights/publications/2021/11/reflections-on-diversity-in-law-firm-pro-bono-practice-management-in-the-uk/.

Chapter 5:
Risk and compliance

By Rebecca Atkinson, director of risk and compliance, Howard Kennedy

Roles in risk and compliance (RC) have significantly increased in the past ten to 15 years. Often the preserve of large Magic Circle or Silver Circle firms, many more firms now have a person or team dedicated to RC. This expansion, alongside the wide variety of work in the RC space, means that it is an attractive career path for many.

This chapter explores what areas of practice RC covers, and how RC teams can be structured, which will illustrate to anyone wanting to start a career in RC where they might sit within a team structure. It also covers the different roles present in the RC space, including those that are required by law or by regulators, and what skills and attributes are needed for such roles. We outline what knowledge is necessary for different areas of RC practice and what qualifications can be gained as well as training that can be undertaken. Finally, we look at some possible career progression routes and what roles might look like in the future.[1]

Areas of practice

RC covers a wide variety of areas of practice, providing great opportunities for those who are interested in broadening their knowledge and experience in a law firm setting. As set out above, RC roles have become more common in law firms, and whilst roles will vary from firm to firm it is useful to understand what areas of practice a role in RC may cover. Below is a non-exhaustive list of practice areas within the RC space:

- Complaint handling.
- Notifications to insurers and claims handling.
- Professional indemnity insurance renewal.
- Data protection compliance, including data subject access requests.
- Cybercrime, often in conjunction with IT.

- Money laundering compliance, to include client due diligence gathering or checking, politically exposed persons, sanctions, and adverse media checking.
- Statutory compliance such as modern slavery, Criminal Finances Act, anti-bribery and corruption, and whistleblowing.
- SRA reauthorization and practicing certificate renewal.
- Code of Conduct queries and in particular conflicts.
- Ethics queries.
- Accounts rules compliance and queries.
- Price transparency rules compliance.
- Gathering and publishing equality and diversity data.
- Ensuring other aspects of compliance are handled, such as information on the firm's letterhead, email, and website.
- Policy writing and ownership.
- Procurement processes.
- Reviewing supplier or outside counsel contracts and/or terms.
- Guidance providing in writing and training.
- Engagement letter and terms of business ownership.
- Business continuity.

How are risk and compliance teams structured in law firms?

It may be useful for those starting their career in RC to understand how teams can be structured. There are many shapes and sizes when it comes to an RC team in a law firm. In some firms, fee earners are given the additional roles that the firm needs to have fulfilled such as COLP, COFA, MLRO, and MLCO (see below for an explanation of these roles) and some firms are fortunate enough to be able to employ people specifically to undertake the RC roles in the firm.

Below are some possible team structures that firms might have. Note though that every firm is different.

A large firm might look like this:

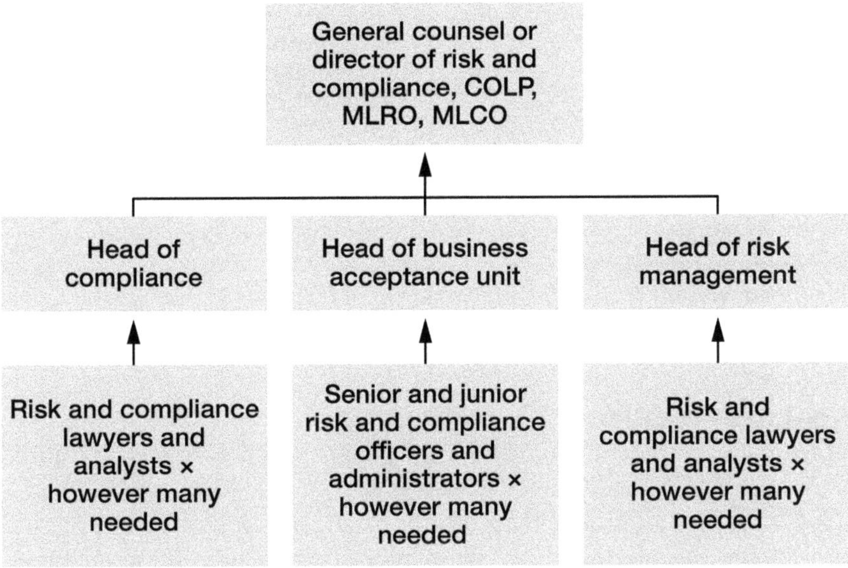

A medium-sized firm might look like this:

A small firm might look like this:

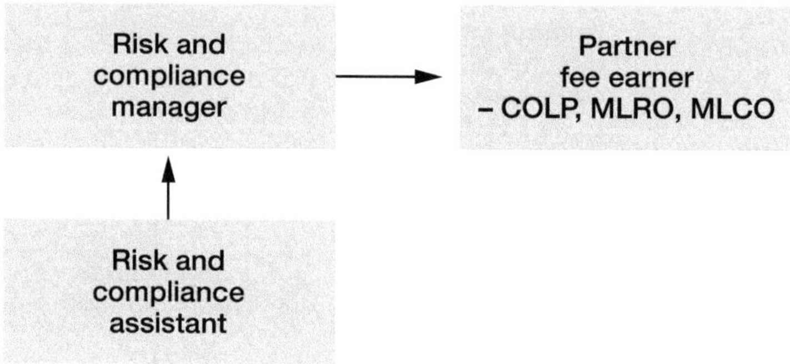

What roles are there?

As seen above, there are many roles in the RC space. Below is an outline of these roles.

Note that job titles and their meaning can vary from firm to firm and save for the roles required by law or regulation there is no requirement for consistency. It is a good idea though for those embarking on a career in RC to ensure their job title aligns with the market so that their job is understood by those in the firm they work, other law firms, and recruiters.

Roles required by law or regulation in England and Wales

These roles can sometimes be standalone full-time roles or be roles undertaken in addition to other roles such as fee earning.

Money laundering reporting officer

Regulation 21(3) of the Money Laundering, Terrorist Financing and Transfer of Funds (Information on the Payer) Regulations 2017 (AML regulations)[2] requires that all practices within the regulated sector must have a "nominated officer" who is tasked with receiving disclosures under Part 7 of the Proceeds of Crime Act 2002 and the Terrorism Act 2000 and to then subsequently make disclosures to the National Crime Agency (NCA). This officer is also known as the money laundering reporting officer (MLRO). If a firm does not provide services within the regulated sector, they do not have to appoint a nominated officer but should consider doing so as good practice.

The MLRO is responsible for ensuring that information that provides knowledge of or suspicion of money laundering is reported to the relevant authority, the NCA, via a Suspicious Activity Report (SAR), and if necessary, a defense sought. The MLRO will also liaise with the NCA and/or police and respond to any queries that they may have, taking into consideration privilege.

This role is a very senior one and carries serious responsibilities. The role requires someone who has the right level of authority to make decisions on when to report to the NCA, independence in their decision-making, and the right resources and amount of time to undertake the role. The MLRO does not have to be a qualified person but is likely to be and in the case of a law firm is often a partner.

It is advisable for the MLRO to nominate a deputy MLRO to assist (particularly in their absence).

For further information about what the Solicitors Regulation Authority (SRA) considers an MLRO must have to be successful in their role, see its guidance "Money Laundering Governance: Three Pillars of Success", published 22 November 2021.[3]

Money laundering compliance officer

Regulation 21(1)(a) of the AML Regulations requires that, where appropriate to the size and nature of the firm's practice, the firm appoints a money laundering compliance officer (MLCO). Therefore, not all firms need to have an MLCO. However, it is likely to be the SRA's expectation that every firm has one unless they are a sole practitioner.

This MLCO is responsible for the firm's compliance with the regulations. This means they are responsible for making sure all policies, controls, and procedures are in place and working. This includes (but is not limited to):

a) Ensuring the firm has conducted a firm-wide risk assessment and that any actions are completed and the risk assessment is regularly reviewed;
b) Ensuring the firm has adequate policies in place and these are adhered to;
c) Ensuring the firm has adequate procedures in place, such as due diligence measures and that these are adhered to;
d) Ensuring that adequate training is provided for relevant staff and that this is done;
e) Ensuring that employees are screened appropriately; and
f) Keeping and maintaining records of high-risk clients and ensuring they are regularly checked.

The Regulations set out that the MLCO needs to be either a member of the board of directors (or if there is no board, of its equivalent management body) or of its senior management. Like the MLRO, the MLCO is often a partner but does not have to be. However, they must be sufficiently senior to make decisions unfettered.

For further information about what the SRA considers an MLCO must have to be successful see its guidance, "Money Laundering Governance: Three Pillars of Success", published 22 November 2021.[4]

Compliance officer for legal practice

All law firms regulated by the SRA must appoint a compliance officer for legal practice (COLP). As set out in Rule 9 of the SRA Code of Conduct for Firms, their role is to:

a) Ensure compliance with the terms and conditions of the firm's authorization;
b) Ensure compliance by the firm and its managers, employees, or interest holders with the SRA's regulatory arrangements that apply to them;
c) Ensure that the firm's managers and interest holders and those they employ or contract with do not cause or substantially contribute to a breach of the SRA's regulatory arrangements;
d) Ensure that a prompt report is made to the SRA of any facts or matters that the COLP reasonably believes is capable of amounting to a serious breach of the terms and conditions of the firm's authorization, or the SRA's regulatory arrangements which apply to the firm, managers, or employees; and
e) Notwithstanding sub-paragraph (d), the COLP must ensure that the SRA is informed promptly of any facts or matters that the COLP reasonably believes should be brought to its attention in order that it may investigate whether a serious breach of its regulatory arrangements has occurred or otherwise exercise its regulatory powers.

The COLP must be a qualified barrister of England and Wales or solicitor of England and Wales. The COLP does not need to be a partner in the firm but often is.

The role of the COLP is a very important one and they are ultimately accountable for compliance in the firm. The COLP can be disciplined if they do not fulfil their role properly. They must have oversight on all activities within the firm to enable them to fulfil their role effectively and therefore it may be a good idea for them to sit on the firm's board or equivalent. Sometimes the COLP will head up the RC function, but not always. For further guidance on the role of COLP, see the Law Society of England and Wales Practice Note Compliance Officers, last updated 14 September 2021.[5]

Compliance officer for finance and administration

All law firms regulated by the SRA must appoint a compliance officer for finance and administration (COFA). As set out in Rule 9 of the SRA Code of Conduct for Firms, their role is to:

a) Ensure that the firm and its managers and employees comply with any obligations imposed upon them under the SRA Accounts Rules;
b) Ensure that a prompt report is made to the SRA of any facts or matters that the COFA reasonably believes is capable of amounting to a serious breach of the SRA Accounts Rules that apply to them; and
c) Notwithstanding sub-paragraph (b), the COFA ensure that the SRA is informed promptly of any facts or matters that they reasonably believe should be brought to its attention in order that it may investigate whether a serious breach of its regulatory arrangements has occurred or otherwise exercise its regulatory powers.

The COFA needs to be someone who is in a position to monitor the firm's compliance with the SRA Accounts Rules and this is often someone with sufficient seniority in the firm's accounts/finance department such as the head of finance or finance director.

How these four roles interact with each other

Let's pause here and look at how the above roles interact with each other. Due to firm size, it is often the case that one individual will take on some or all of the above roles. These roles certainly overlap and if undertaken by more than one person can provide an environment of support amongst role holders.

It is the MLRO's decision whether there exists suspicion or knowledge such that a report to the NCA needs to be made by the MLRO. The MLCO will want to make sure that everyone in the firm knows when to report suspicions to the MLRO. This will also be of interest to the COLP, who has responsibility for ensuring compliance with all regulatory arrangements.

In the scenario of a money laundering concern, the COFA will want to be sure that the non-banking rule (r3.3) of the SRA Accounts Rules has not been breached.

If an accounts rules breach does occur, the COFA will need to consider if this should result in a report to the SRA, which will be of interest and concern to the COLP. Further, if the accounts rule breach has raised money laundering suspicions, this needs to be reported to the MLRO.

Data protection officer

Under the UK GDPR, firms must appoint a data protection officer (DPO) if:

- Their core activities require large-scale, regular and systematic monitoring of individuals (for example, online behavior tracking); or
- Their core activities consist of large-scale processing of special categories of data or data relating to criminal convictions and offences.

Firms can choose to have a DPO on a voluntary basis if they do not consider they meet the criteria.

The DPO needs to be someone who is able to dedicate time to the role and who ideally has knowledge of data protection laws. The DPO's role is to be the first point of contact for any data protection activities. They should be senior within the firm.

The DPO's tasks are defined in Article 39 GDPR as:

- To inform and advise the firm about its obligations to comply with the GDPR and other data protection laws;
- To monitor compliance with the GDPR and other data protection laws, and with the firm's data protection polices, including managing internal data protection activities, raising awareness of data protection issues, training staff, and conducting internal audits;
- To advise on, and to monitor, data protection impact assessments;
- To cooperate with the supervisory authority; and
- To be the first point of contact for supervisory authorities and for individuals whose data is processed (employees, customers etc.).

The Information Commissioner's guidance[6] sets out that it is important to remember that the DPO's tasks cover all personal data processing activities, not just those that require their appointment under Article 37(1) of the GDPR. In its guidance the ICO states:

- *When carrying out their tasks the DPO is required to take into account the risk associated with the processing the firm is undertaking. They must have regard to the nature, scope, context and purposes of the processing.*
- *The DPO should prioritize and focus on the more risky activities, for example where special category data is being processed, or where the potential impact on individuals could be damaging. Therefore, DPOs should provide risk-based advice to the firm.*

Depending on the size of the firm there may be other data protection roles that firms want or need to have in place and the firm may wish to appoint a deputy DPO.

Other officers – whistleblowing and anti-bribery and corruption

Whistleblowing (disclosure, usually by an employee, of activity that may be criminal) can provide an important method of obtaining information about activity that needs to be investigated. It is therefore important for those in a firm to know who to whistleblow to. Firms may therefore decide to appoint a whistleblowing officer. This person may also be responsible for the firm's whistleblowing policy and training.

The same applies to anti-bribery and corruption. Firms may wish to appoint an anti-bribery and corruption officer for people to report concerns to. As above, this person can also be responsible for the firm's anti-bribery and corruption policy and training.

Senior level roles

- **General counsel**. The general counsel (GC) used to be the preserve of Magic Circle firms, but in more recent times the role of the GC is being seen in firms that, although sizeable, are not as large as those in the Magic Circle. Like many roles in law firms, the GC role can differ from firm to firm. Generally speaking, however, the GC is a lawyer who will often oversee the RC function (normally when a firm has a GC there is a RC team also), set the strategic plans for RC in the firm, and also advise the firm's board or equivalent on all legal and regulatory aspects of firm practice. A GC can come from various different backgrounds. Historically, a GC is someone who has been a practicing solicitor, either practicing in commercial law or litigation, and often as a partner in a law firm. There is a new breed of GC that has not come from this practicing background but from different RC roles or regulators or other businesses. The GC may also be the MLRO, MLCO, COLP, and/or COFA. The GC may lead on internal and regulatory investigations, claims and PI renewal.

- **Director of risk and compliance**. Generally speaking, a director of risk and compliance, like the GC, will oversee the RC function and set the strategic plans for RC in the firm. The director of risk and compliance may also be the MLRO, MLCO, COLP, and/or COFA but they will not generally advise the firm's board or equivalent on all legal and regulatory aspects of firm practice. Often the director will take on more of a strategic role than an operational one and advise key stakeholders in the firm about matters of RC. The director of risk and compliance may lead on internal and regulatory investigations, claims, and PI renewal. A director of risk and compliance does not have to be a qualified person but is likely to have many years' experience. Firms of a certain size may have both a GC and director of risk and compliance.
- **Head of risk and compliance or risk and compliance manager**. Ordinarily, a head of risk and compliance or risk and compliance manager will oversee the RC function and a head of risk and compliance may be the firm's MLRO, MLCO, COLP, and/or COFA (but a manager level person would not normally undertake those roles). Often the head or manager will have an operational role line managing those in the RC team. They may set the RC agenda or may take the firm's agenda from others such as director or GC. The head or manager may handle complaints or claims, general day-to-day queries or any of the tasks outlined in the next role below. A head of risk and compliance does not have to be a qualified person but is likely to have many years' experience. A risk and compliance manager also does have to be a qualified person and may have less experience than a head of risk and compliance.

Operational roles

- **Risk and compliance lawyer or advisor**. Often this role will be advisory to the firm and may deal with complaints, notifications to insurers, and claims, and general RC queries about the Codes of Conduct, ethics, money laundering, data protection, and other regulatory requirements. This person may produce written guidance, provide training, and induct new people into the firm. This person may or may not be legally qualified (i.e., solicitor, barrister, CILEX or other). They may have many years' experience or be trained on the job.

- **Business acceptance manager or head.** The business acceptance team is in place to on-board all of the firm's clients by undertaking due diligence checks. This is normally done through a series of on-boarding platforms and tools or could be more manual, such as checking identification documents and undertaking research via open sources. A manager or head will oversee this function and manage those people within the team.
- **Risk and compliance analyst or paralegal**. This role can vary significantly depending on the firm. Often an analyst role will focus on client on-boarding (due diligence, politically exposed person, sanction, and adverse media checking) but not always. This role could provide assistance and guidance to those in the firm on a wide range of issues such as money laundering, complaints, Code of Conduct queries, ethics and so on. Often this role does not require the person to be qualified and the person may have many years' experience or be trained on the job.
- **Risk and compliance officer**. This role is often very similar to the analyst role and can be concentrated on client on-boarding (due diligence, politically exposed person, sanction, and adverse media checking). The role could contain other tasks also that do not center on client on-boarding and this will depend on the firm's needs. This role does not require the person to be qualified and is a great entry level role for those who are starting out in RC.
- **Risk and compliance administrator or assistant**. Often this role is to provide administrative support to the RC team or the firm in terms of filing, recording information, and taking on any administrative tasks such as arranging meetings, training and so on. This role does not require the person to be qualified and is a great entry level role for those who are starting out in RC.

What skills and attributes are needed for roles in risk and compliance?

Attributes are qualities that people might naturally have. Skills are things people have learnt through work, training or education, or life experience. The skills and attributes that are often needed for a role in RC will depend on the role itself. Here are some that may be needed:

- Active listening;
- Adaptability;
- Analytical thinking;
- Assertiveness;
- Attention to detail;
- Collaboration;
- Communication;
- Confidence;
- Conflict resolution;
- Consistency;
- Creative thinking and thinking outside the box;
- Data analysis;
- Decision making;
- Emotional intelligence;
- Hardworking and diligent;
- Independence;
- Leadership;
- Managing difficult conversations;
- Motivational;
- Multitasking;
- Persuasion;
- Positivity and a "can do" attitude;
- Proactive and self-sufficient;
- Fast-acting when need arises;
- Reading comprehension;
- Relationship building;

- Report writing;
- Research;
- Resilience;
- Respectfulness;
- Responsible, accountable, and dependable;
- Strategic thinking skills;
- Teamwork; and
- Working under pressure.

What knowledge and qualifications are needed and what training can be undertaken?

The knowledge that is needed for an RC role will naturally depend on the role itself. Some roles are advertised as entry level and do not require any prior knowledge. For roles that require knowledge this will depend on the tasks of the role. Generally speaking, persons could be expected to have the following knowledge:

- **MLRO and MLCO** – understanding of the AML Regulations and the Legal Sector Affinity Group guidance.
- **COLP** – understanding of the SRA COLP regime to include reporting requirements, the Codes of Conduct, and a broad understanding of other legal and regulatory requirements that are placed on firms.
- **COFA** – understanding of the SRA COFA regime to include reporting requirements and the SRA Accounts Rules.
- **Director, head, manager, lawyer, advisor** – these people will need to have a broad understanding of the legal and regulatory requirements that are placed on firms.
- **For roles that center on client on-boarding** – an understanding of the AML Regulations and the Legal Sector Affinity Group guidance, an understanding of how to undertake checks for politically exposed persons, sanctions, and adverse media, and what the results mean. Some firms may require the person to understand the sanctions regime.

Some roles require the person to be a qualified lawyer (solicitor or barrister) as outlined above (e.g., the COLP and risk and compliance lawyer).

There are very few RC qualifications. The most popular are qualifications through the International Compliance Association (ICA)[7] with more and more junior RC people undertaking an employer-funded qualification through this company. Training webinars, events, and materials in the RC space are vast and often free. Here are some of the places to look for free training and guidance:

- The Law Society of England and Wales.
- The SRA often provide free content and every year they hold a free COLP and COFA conference. The SRA also has its own YouTube channel where content is stored[8] and a compliance update that can be signed up to.[9]
- Legal Risk LLP provides very useful content and anyone is able to sign up to its newsletter.[10]
- Law firms often provide free webinars and they can be searched for on the internet.
- Suppliers who have tech products to sell often provide free content, webinars, and events.
- Training suppliers often provide free content as well as very good training to purchase. VinciWorks is one example.[11]

Career progression routes

As can be seen above, there are a number of different roles in RC with varying qualification, knowledge, and skills requirements. It is highly possible for someone to enter into the RC space in a non-qualified capacity and rise up the team structure through gaining experience, knowledge, and qualifications. For example, someone could begin as a risk and compliance officer or administrator and, with good progression, a few years' hard work, and dedication, become a client on-boarding manager or head of business acceptance.

Some roles do require qualification and so non-qualified people will not be able to undertake them. However, this should not deter anyone from wanting to start their career in RC. Firms are often keen to develop their own people and, with the SQE, the ability to become qualified is more accessible.

Practicing solicitors or other types of fee earners are also able to transition to an RC role, especially given their knowledge of the SRA regulatory regime, areas of legal practice, and other aspects such as client care. Some fee earners may be able to apply for a role in RC without any prior experience, but if a lack of experience is preventing this career progression, then the fee earner may wish to consider lending the RC team a hand, if possible, perhaps in considering a complaint on behalf of the firm, handling a negligence claim, or writing a policy or some guidance. Those wishing to transition into an RC role may also wish to consider undertaking courses, attending events, and reading widely on RC topics.

What does the future look like?

Firms are investing more and more into RC personnel. This is due to recognition of the importance of the RC function and also because regulators are becoming stricter and the stakes higher.

In many firms, RC teams have got larger and will continue to grow. The role of the GC has become more common and risk and compliance officer positions often prove a fantastic entry into an RC career with on-the-job training as well as employer-funded training. The future will see a further expansion of these roles, which will not decrease in number.

References

1. Please note this chapter is written from the perspective of risk and compliance requirements in England.
2. www.legislation.gov.uk/uksi/2017/692/contents/made
3. www.sra.org.uk/sra/research-report/money-laundering-governance-three-pillars-of-success/
4. *Ibid.*
5. www.lawsociety.org.uk/en/topics/business-management/compliance-officers
6. https://ico.org.uk/for-organisations/guide-to-data-protection/guide-to-the-general-data-protection-regulation-gdpr/accountability-and-governance/data-protection-officers/#ib7
7. www.int-comp.org/
8. www.youtube.com/user/SRAsolicitors
9. www.sra.org.uk/sra/news/sra-update/
10. www.legalrisk.co.uk/
11. https://vinciworks.com/

Chapter 6: How to create a successful career in legal business development

By Anne Macdonald, partner and head of business development, Harper Macleod LLP

We all know that clients are the lifeblood of every legal firm. We need to grow to in effect stand still and achieve the same results as the previous month, therefore a continual stream of new instructions – whether that be from existing clients or new clients – is a must. This brings squarely into focus the need for every law firm to focus on and prioritize business development.

How do you embed a culture of business development throughout your firm?

The term business development is often associated exclusively with selling and that's a word that sparks fear in a lot of lawyers! But actually I think business development is simply about building relationships and that is something that all lawyers are very good at, each in their own unique way. For some, relationship building, the art of the conversation, and ability to cross-refer come naturally, but I certainly do not subscribe to the school of thought that relationship building should be solely the preserve of the rainmakers within a firm – it is about collective responsibility. Every law firm thrives upon good client relationships and strengthening those and growing new relationships is simply part of the eco-system of a legal business. Everyone has a part to play. Every touch point a client (or a prospective client) has with the firm is a chance to impress and leave an indelible mark on the client's perception of the client care. Therefore, whether you are a paralegal, trainee, receptionist, cashier, business development executive, marketing executive, partner, or associate it matters not a jot; we are all ambassadors for the firm and every interaction needs to be a good one.

In my view there is also no right or wrong approach to business development – it has to sit comfortably with each of us in order for it to be authentic and engaging. Not all have the natural skillset or desire to undertake business development activities such as pitches, coffees, delivering webinars, making direct approaches or setting up referral relationships. However, I often think that the technical lawyer, who would rather just get on with their work and is known as the go-to in that area of law because of the respect garnered over the years for such good work, is an excellent example of business development. The fact that so many clients are happy with their work and other lawyers defer to them for second opinions makes them a great asset and indirectly they are doing very good business development for the firm!

I do find the term "rainmaker" rather divisive and cringe worthy; it celebrates the winning of client instructions at an individual level rather than the team effort that will absolutely have been at play. Yes, there are standout lawyers and business development professionals who raise the profile of the firm and bring in work but to single them out as rainmakers pays a disservice to the team members who are keeping the plates spinning whilst others are out "winning" work. Furthermore, it can have a polarizing effect as for anyone that feels nervous about business development activities, the constant comparison to the celebrated rainmakers can be demotivating and can lead to low morale. The term rainmaker is largely a consequence of "eat what you kill" remuneration structures and feels like an outdated concept.

So, business development is very much about playing to the strengths of all within your firm. If one of your lawyers is displaying standout business development, team player, and relationship building skills, would you consider encouraging them to focus on that and hang up the client advisory (dare I say, fee earning) role? And how do you put in place structures to allow those within the firm with a talent and flair for business development to carve out a career path focused on just that?

Making the switch

A decade ago, switching from a client-facing solicitor role to create a business development team was a rare and eyebrow-raising career move. Fast forward to 2022 and it's far more commonplace. I've had the pleasure of getting to know some of the early movers and will share the experiences of Rachel Hussey – client and markets partner, Arthur Cox; Stuart Cartwright – partner, JMW; and Kat Rozenbaum – head of business development, Mishcon de Reya LLP throughout this chapter:

It speaks volumes about the management culture and inclusive approach at a law firm when alternative roles to fee earning are embraced and encouraged. For Rachel Hussey, when she joined Arthur Cox in early

2000 to set up the marketing and business development team, it was a novel move. Rachel had enjoyed a very successful legal career but began to experience the imbalance created between what she wanted to achieve at home with a young family and what she wanted to achieve at work and therefore was motivated to look at an alternative legal career. Such roles did not exist in Ireland at the time, and much like Stuart and Kat's experience, eyebrows were raised. The arching of brows did not last long though as very quickly the unique perspective that a seasoned lawyer can bring to the business development and client relationship strategy of a firm was plain to see. A pivotal moment for Rachel was her promotion to partner in 2007, followed by appointment to the management committee, such is the importance and value afforded to business development and client relations within Arthur Cox.

Stuart Cartwright is very clear that when Joy Kingsley, senior partner at JMW, approached him with the offer of launching and heading up the Lawshare network back in 2010, it was not a cheap decision for the firm – it was taking a high performing partner out of a team. The firm recognized the relationship building talents that Stuart had and the importance of investing in business development. For Stuart, he was excited by the prospect but recalls vividly how scary it felt to be giving up his files and security blanket of what he knew and turning up to a new desk with a blank screen on the computer.

For me, as a newly qualified solicitor during the credit crunch of 2008 and in a secure role with Harper Macleod LLP, it was a leap of faith to turn my attention to business development full-time. The firm recognized something in me and in that moment I truly saw what a place of opportunity Harper Macleod is. At a time when redundancies were being made and a trimming of resources, the firm embraced investing in my future aspirations to create a business development team and run a legal referral network. It was a first in the Scottish legal market at the time. It was a brave move by the management team and, on reflection, by me too. I was able to shine in the role because of the very fact it was fully supported by the firm and from the start I reported directly to our chief executive.

It's most definitely the cultural mind-set that is the major inhibitor of firms – you still occasionally hear the phrase "fee earner versus fee burner" being touted about. The misapprehension is that business support is an overhead and everyday rhetoric such as "Oh you've now become a cost". It's a sentiment that acted as a motivator for Kat when she made the switch, determined to "prove the naysayers wrong and show that I absolutely was not a cost, I was an income generator". For Stuart, the validation of his decision to make the switch is all in the data; an individual billing target for a salaried criminal partner was likely in the region of £200k back in 2010; he is now a board member who presides over a team that generates what he describes as "significant revenue" for the firm from referrals and new business.

The benefits of bringing legal experience to business development

A colleague of mine often laments that generally in life there are three types of law firms – some that are great at marketing, some who do fabulous quality of work, and only a few that do both! Now wouldn't it be great if more firms could fall into the latter category? There has been an historic mismatch at times between the marketing and client advisory teams within law firms and this is why a business development team with a background in law and practice might just be the answer.

So what is it that a lawyer turned business development professional brings to the table? For me, it's the fact that I have been there, done that – when you have spent a good part of your lifetime recording you know just how precious every six minutes of a solicitor's time is. I do think this is why a solicitor turned business development professional has an innate perspective and understanding of the pressures faced by the client advisory teams within their law firm. On the flip side, they also know the "excuses" that are so often used to brush off doing business development activities.

For Kat Rozenbaum, it's the legal training, strategic mind, and experience of being involved in deal making that are the standout qualities that a lawyer brings to the business development table. If you are going to take up someone's time, whether it's an internal colleague, existing client, or prospect, you need to be well prepared – do your research, identify the issues, and then use your judgement to implement solutions. The understanding of what clients pay for and what clients want allows you to maximize the value of what the firm can deliver to them. It's what Kat likes to call hybrid BD – you bring a legal mind-set and ability to ensure seamless client service combined with people skills and you have the winning formula.

The umbrella view of the firm and clients that you can take in a business development role is hugely important for Rachel, for whom it's a whole firm approach. The executive teams do not talk about "my client" or "my file" or "my win"; rather it's working towards the common goal of business success. Every action taken is firm-centric – how will this help the bottom line, how will this enhance the brand, how will this help clients, how will this help client advisors in delivering legal services. I think it is here that one finds a very important distinction in mind-set between business development by solicitors at an individual or team level, and business development by a dedicated business development professional who is able to take a more strategic view of business development activity across the firm.

The hugely positive stakeholder engagement that can be harnessed by having a dedicated business development partner in terms of client engagement cannot be underestimated. When I go out to talk to clients, the fact that I'm a partner makes a big difference to them – first in being happy to see me, but also then realizing that the firm takes client feedback and client relationships seriously enough to have a partner dealing with it.

Kat recently had a chat with a former senior partner of a leading City firm regarding his approach to legal business development. He bluntly, yet perfectly, hit the nail on the head with, "Does it generate revenue and/or does it massage egos?" If you can't answer "yes" to at least one of those, don't do it.

What about career paths?

As a lawyer there is a well-worn path from trainee to NQ, associate to partner. When you move to a business development role, do you follow that same path? I'm happy to say that for Stuart, Rachel, Kat, and myself, that's exactly what has happened and that is very much a testament to each of our firms. I've been adamant that this legacy should continue and that all within the business development team at my firm, Harper Macleod, should continue on their legal career paths. As it stands, amongst eight of the team members, six are lawyers at various stages from partner to associate, all with current practicing certificates. However, not all within a business development team will have a law degree. It's so important that there are distinct career paths mapped out to ensure meaningful progression. For Rachel, that means developing a roadmap from assistant to executive to manager and director and creating a comprehensive strategized system to allow tangible progress for all.

All around us a war for talent is pervading. The firms that retain talent and take an expansive approach to inclusion are the firms that will continue to flourish. For Kat, it's simple – before we lose associates to other industries or professions, we should make room to nurture the potential that they have. After all, the knowledge that an associate has amassed about the firm and people within it, the clients and introducer relationships, is a very important asset and firms would do well to retain such talent albeit in a different role.

So, if you'd like to make the move into a dedicated business development role, where do you look for such opportunities? The first port of call should be your current firm – consider the structure and shape of the firm. Does it have a dedicated business development and marketing department? If so, then some early conversations with the director of business development and marketing would be sensible. If not, then why not create a business case/plan to present to your management team to explain why setting up a solicitor-led business development team would be an asset to the firm. Perhaps, you see making the switch to business development as a catalyst to join a new firm and if that is the case then LinkedIn is a good place to start to consider the opportunities in the legal marketplace. Registering with a dedicated recruitment agency will ensure that you hear about quality and prestigious business development roles that are available.

You have to see it to be it

It's also important to have a role model; someone to look up to who has walked the path you'd like to take. If you don't see that then you may struggle to visualize what it means to succeed as a legal business development professional. It is all very well being a trailblazer but it is of comfort to know that successful career paths have been forged by those before you. In the early stages of my career, I'd look to Elliot Moss and Julia Hayhoe who were (and still are) the leading lights in legal business development and strategy and held management group positions.[1] It was so inspiring for me to see that you could absolutely reach leadership roles within law firms without following a traditional legal career. There is now a wider choice of such role models as firms begin to embrace a range of alternative legal careers and recognize the value in involving a more diverse group in managerial decision making.

Lessons learned?

Making the switch has allowed me to become much more attuned to the unhelpful and at times demeaning terminology that is used within law firms. It's only when you are sitting in someone else's chair that you begin to realize the impact certain commonly used phrases – "non-fee earner" being the main culprit – has. We only learn when we look at the world through the eyes of another instead of conforming to legacy norms.

For Rachel, it was a simple solution – she banned the use of such phrases within Arthur Cox over a decade ago so perhaps it's time the rest of us caught up. I am as guilty as the next of using such language. I previously would routinely describe myself as a "non-fee earning solicitor". It had become ingrained language and I really needed to make a conscious effort not to describe myself in that way. A business development colleague and friend through the IBA, Katherine Hutchison, called such rhetoric out in a very pragmatic way: do you hear of non-doctors, non-dentists, non-chefs or non-pilots?[2] It's a powerful analogy. Simply put, we should use the correct titles for our colleagues, focusing on what they do, not what they don't do; so "business development solicitor" instead of "non-fee earning solicitor" for example. Everyone has an identity and no one should be branded as a "non". Rachel goes further here, and even the very commonly utilized term in law firms of "business support" or "centralized support" doesn't sit well. It has connotations of a propping up or a subordinate role rather than the dynamic, proactive leadership and direction that highly qualified and talented business development and executive teams actually provide.

Conclusion

Taking on the role of business development solicitor is a liberating experience. It allows you to develop a bird's eye view of the firm and immerse yourself in and provide direction on the strategic aims of the firm and its key clients. It allows you to truly become part of the business of your law firm, to spend time researching and learning about emerging markets and sectors and to network with the business community. It will enhance your profile internally and externally and in doing so sets your firm apart from others that have more traditional structures and outlooks on legal life.

Like Arthur Cox, JMW, and Mishcon de Reya, Harper Macleod is a leader in this regard and roles within our collective business development teams are much sought after, attracting an extremely high caliber of candidate. The team is well respected within the firm and has become indispensable to the client advisory teams. The firm culture is such that there's no hint of a suggestion that business development solicitors are not "real" solicitors. The leadership team mirrors this respectful behavior, demonstrating how valued the team is through recognition of business development achievements in internal communications, pay reviews, promotions and appointments within business development and putting the team forward for awards. Simply put, the business development solicitors are treated as equals.

For those who have the right skills, a career in business development may well prove more fulfilling than the traditional solicitor career path and

I would encourage anyone who is interested in exploring that possibility to go for it.

References

1. Elliot is currently a partner and chief brand officer at Mishcon de Reya and for the last decade has been an influential name in legal BD due to the senior positions he has held within Mishcon and the fact that he has always been so kind with his time, sharing best practice at legal BD conferences and chairing panel sessions. I remember at the inaugural Lawyer Law Firm Management Awards in 2012 being shortlisted in the final three for Best Business Development team alongside Elliot and his team and Julia's team at Baker McKenzie – personally, that was a pivotal moment for me! And who won, you might be asking? Well, it was Julia and her team at Baker McKenzie. What I admire most about Julia is her ability to curate and implement truly transformative projects within the legal sector. At Baker McKenzie, Julia was latterly the global chief strategy officer and global executive committee member. Advising and working with four successive chairmen and leadership teams over 12 years, Julia led strategic growth, leadership, and business transformation projects. Prior to that Julia was the director of marketing, business development and communications, and if you saw Julia's name as a speaker at a conference or that she had written an article, you booked to attend or bookmarked the article as you just knew how much sense would be conveyed.
2. Anne Macdonald, "Law firm success – the (not so) secret ingredient? Your executive team," *Modern Lawyer*, Globe Law and Business, April 2021.

Chapter 7: The shifting sands in talent management

By Rachel Brushfield, founder, EnergiseLegal

Introduction

What shifting sands in the last two years!

This chapter explores the careers and roles in law firm HR and talent management, qualifications and routes in, emerging in-demand skills, and what candidates need to do to brand, market, and network for career success.

COVID-19 and all the rapid accelerated change that it meant for law firms has finally got HR and talent practitioners the recognition that they deserve. HR were at the heart of business agility throughout the lockdowns, adapting many strategies and processes. A decade of change happened in one year, and for the legal profession, historically a traditional profession, these changes were much needed.

> *"It is a really exciting time to be in HR/talent management. Law firms have realized that this is a business-critical role. Sustainable success is all about your people. It is great to see HR talent finally getting the recognition that they so deserve. Firms need to ensure that they invest in HR talent to attract, develop and retain the best, especially with a talent shortage."*
> **Laura McNair**, Head of HR and operations practice, Totum & Partners.[1]

Impact of COVID-19

Human Resources has grown up. It now has a seat at the top table. Originally called "Personnel", HR used to do the tasks that solicitors didn't want to do. But HR kept the wheels turning during the global COVID-19 pandemic, introducing home working, providing wellbeing support to staff, and much more. The shifting sands have moved from policies and processes to people. People are, after all, at the heart of professional services.

The landscape of talent has changed since COVID-19 and will no doubt change further. The shift to remote and hybrid working, for example, means that firms, especially against the backdrop of a talent shortage in HR, can recruit candidates from other geographical areas away from the firm's office location. Openness to part-time instead of full-time working has also shifted. A whole new pool of talent – part-time workers, of which there are many talented people from different generations – has emerged. Law firms are now open to part-time roles of three days a week for the right person with the right skills, knowledge, and experience who fits their culture. There is still a preference to come to the office, but not necessarily every day. The presentism obsession has been partially dissolved.

Careers and role options

Talent management encompasses a wide range of roles, including workforce planning, talent management, change management, employer branding, and diversity and inclusion. What the roles are called and which department they sit in depends on the firm. They can sit in Human Resources, recruitment, operations, change management, or business transformation. An explanation of each of these roles is provided below:

- Workforce planning is the strategic practice of understanding the composition of your workforce and how the different departments interlink. It is a role that gives a bird's eye view of the firm's people, the interlinks between the departments, and can identify the opportunity for both creating new teams and redesigning roles to better meet client needs in a fast changing world.
- Talent management refers to the anticipation of required human capital for a firm and the planning to meet those needs. A role in talent management involves the methodically organized and strategic process of getting the right talent onboard and helping them grow to their optimal capabilities, keeping the firm's organizational objectives in mind. In larger firms, there will be different roles in the talent management department, looking after and responsible for different segments of the firm's talent pool, e.g., graduates, associates, business support staff etc. Talent development is a subset of talent management, focusing on helping talent to develop, grow, and achieve their potential, e.g., via webinars, executive coaching, leadership development programs etc.
- Change management is an interesting and business-critical role in a law firm as we live in fast changing and uncertain times where change is essential to survive and thrive. Lawyers are trained to

be risk averse, so understanding the emotional aspects of change, resistance to it, and how to overcome this are as important as the tools and models to enable it.

- Employer branding is a role that involves marketing the firm as a brand to the external target audience of target employees to attract them to want to work at the firm, rather than choose a competitor. It involves developing a strategy to communicate the firm as a desirable place to work, the employee value proposition – what is in it for the candidate to work there – and the employee experience journey, from recruitment, through on-boarding/induction and beyond. Parallels with marketing the firm as a corporate brand to its clients means that candidates with a marketing and communications career heritage may move into an employer brand role with their relevant transferable knowledge and experience.
- Diversity and inclusion (D+I), or equality, diversity, and inclusion (EDI) as it is often called, is ensuring that the firm considers talent from all sources. Private practice has traditionally sourced lawyers from the top universities for example, with women, ethnic minorities, people with disabilities, and talent from underprivileged backgrounds being underrepresented. A role in diversity and inclusion requires the development of a strategy and plan to ensure fairness and to engage key stakeholders to make it happen in reality, setting targets and monitoring progress. Environmental, social, and governance (ESG) is an emerging hybrid evolution of D+I/corporate social responsibility.[2]

Current growth areas in talent management are diversity and inclusion, including specialisms within it such as intergenerational working and, as we emerge from the COVID-19 pandemic, recruitment roles to build up staffing for sustainable success and growth. As competition for recruiting staff grows in the war for talent, it is likely that specialist roles such as employer branding and the employee value proposition and experience will grow, especially in larger firms.

The ability to think in an integrated, strategic way and see the link between strategy (the legal market), business (systems, processes, culture), and people (talent) within organizational development is essential. Law firms need to question themselves about their own outdated bias regarding recruiting talent: *"Do we really need to recruit someone with a law firm background?"* Perhaps someone from a different background may bring useful new perspectives to help shift the sands of talent management further.

Law firms need to invest in attracting and developing HR talent to attract and keep the cream of the crop. Historically, firms have prioritized the development of fee earners, but the people who look after people – HR – are important too. COVID-19 has put the spotlight on this. What would have happened during the first lockdown without HR in place does not bear thinking about.

Larger law firms are likely to have more specialist roles within a bigger department. Once you have joined the firm, you have more scope to broaden your skills and knowledge internally by making internal rather than external moves.

How to choose your HR talent specialism

Self-awareness and knowledge is vital to decide the right career path for you. What motivates and interests you? Is it diversity and inclusion or ESG? Workforce planning, change management, wellbeing, the employer brand to attract talent to the firm? Perhaps it is recruitment – the process of getting the right people at the right time on the right terms to join the firm – or the employee value proposition – segmenting employees into smaller groupings and working out what they want for a compelling relationship that builds the psychological contract, that unspoken relationship between employee and employer about what is given in effort versus what is received in reward and engagement.

If your role is to be recruiting lawyers, it is useful to have been a lawyer, because you have and will be perceived to have career experience of what it is like and the recruitment journey and its touchpoints. Likewise, if graduate recruitment is your area of interest, recently going through the graduate recruitment journey and experience is beneficial.

Qualifications and routes into talent management

The Chartered Institute of Personnel Development (CIPD),[3] the membership organization for HR professionals, offers qualifications that are a common starting point into HR as a career. There are various CIPD qualifications and membership levels up to Fellow.[4] The CIPD profession map[5] lays out a clear CPD path and how to achieve it – it includes core knowledge, behaviors, and specialist knowledge and is outcome-focused.

Some examples of routes into talent management are:

- Partners who pivot their careers into training and development, often those that have especially enjoyed the training and development aspects of the partner role;

- Working at a law school as a steppingstone e.g., working as a lecturer or CPD teacher, then moving into a law firm;
- Moving from fee earning into a recruitment agency, then in-house recruitment followed by a broader resourcing role;
- Employment lawyers with their strong connection with people, the world of work, and talent can move into human capital roles; and
- A natural aptitude for business development can also lead into a career move into talent management. It is a different kind of growth and acquisition, in the human capital rather than client space.

Making an internal career move

With internal career moves within a law firm, having a sponsor can really help to make a move a reality, as well as being skilled at managing and influencing stakeholders. An awareness of how talent is defined in your own firm, how and when decisions are made, as well as finding a solution for your manager for the gap that you will leave in their team when you leave helps.

Volunteering to be part of a committee, for example diversity and inclusion, broadens experience and is a useful toe in the water for whether a career in this area appeals in reality rather than in theory.

Emerging in-demand skills to perform talent roles

Specific emerging competencies for HR are:

- Commercial awareness;
- The strategic ability to see the big picture and link between people and the firm's business strategy;
- Internal coaching; and
- Data analytics, in order to prepare business cases to justify programs and investment.

Commercial awareness is the knowledge of how businesses make money, what clients want, and what problems there are in a particular area of business. Being comfortable with numbers and using data and facts to prepare business cases is an important element of commercial awareness.

Business support staff can still be perceived as not adding as much value as fee earners, so the ability to demonstrate the value you bring is important and it is essential that you understand the drivers of value in business if you are on the senior leadership team.

In-demand skills and knowledge that will emerge in the future will include artificial intelligence (AI) and machine learning, and a holistic view of workforce planning, which includes people and robots/machines.

Artificial intelligence or AI is a useful emerging technology that helps Human Resources to recruit, measure, reward, and develop people. Increasingly, AI will become integrated into Human Resources. AI's value is in analysing, predicting, and diagnosing information to enable HR to make better decisions and deploy resources in a more accurate and timely way. Two examples of practical applications of AI include analysing employee referrals to understand what works best, and analysing a job candidate's experience and skills and their match to current advertised roles.

In a nutshell, AI automates repetitive tasks, gives HR data-backed resources and insights gathered directly from employees, freeing them up to add more value with more time for strategic and creative tasks, e.g., horizon scanning for future talent needs to ensure a sustainable competitive advantage for the firm.

Marketing, branding, and networking in the talent management space

LinkedIn is the most important platform for HR professionals to network. Knowing the right key words for your human capital specialism will help you to attract recruiters and potential employers. Knowing the "language" and the hot topics is important.

Your network speaks volumes about you. This is visible on LinkedIn via your connections. Visibility is key, so liking and commenting on relevant posts, following key influencers, and creating your own content is all worth making time for.

Attending face to face and online events and conferences and becoming a member of specialist networks, especially as you become more senior, is key. CIPD, for example, has national conferences and regional groups where you can broaden your network.

Networking for junior–mid level HR

Aside from CIPD, networks such as the Chartered Management Institute[6] and Changeboard[7] also have useful events to help individuals understand the roles and build knowledge. Many employment law departments in firms also have events, so this is an opportunity to meet peers from other sectors and share learning and best practice. Connecting with everyone you meet at events broadens and deepens your network, and builds your career capital, something that is vital in the digital age.

Keeping up to date with industry developments is achieved by subscribing to various online and printed publications as well as keeping an eye on who is winning awards and what for. Volunteering as a committee member for your local CIPD group can be a useful way to create visibility and meet useful contacts, paving the way for your next career move.

Blocking out time to read high quality articles and white papers (e.g., *Harvard Business Review*, Hay, Henley Management School, PwC, Deloitte etc.) is also worthwhile.

Networking for senior HR

Joining the Managing Partner's Forum (MPF) "People Performance and Culture Group"[8] and/or Winmark's "Chief HR Officer" network[9] are useful actions to take for high quality networking with senior people. MPF has a special interest group, "Knowledge and learning", which I found useful and interesting. There is a CIPD network for senior HR members, "Senior leaders network"[10] and various invitation-only networks for senior HR professionals where you need to be in the know to be invited!

My path into talent management[11]

My own route into talent management involved taking a six-month self-funded Continual Professional Development break and immersing myself in it. I became an affiliate member of the CIPD, which I found invaluable, reading the various research reports and articles that it publishes and articles in its *People Management* magazine, attending relevant annual CIPD conferences, plus CIPD forums on various topics at the CIPD head office in Wimbledon. I also joined my local branch of CIPD and served on the committee for a year.

Learning the language of talent management was important. I found that interviewing experts in law firms for an article I was writing was a great multi-benefit approach. I would feel comfortable approaching them, they would be happy to be approached and interviewed for their expertise and be quoted in an article, and introduce me to other useful contacts in their network. There was also the tangible and satisfying outcome of a printed article with my name and company name Energise on it, which I could use in marketing my services and have a downloadable PDF on my website.

I built up my knowledge and confidence, learning best practice, expanding my network and embedded knowledge on an ongoing basis by writing blogs, articles, and books, and running events. I also joined relevant LinkedIn groups. Together, undertaking these activities resulted in my successful career pivot into talent management.

Summary and conclusions

HR has arrived! Due to COVID-19, it has gained the respect, credibility, and gravitas that it deserves in law firms. Its contribution and deserved place at the top table in making business-critical decisions about human resourcing has been recognized as a result of COVID-19 and all the changes that this has caused; disruption of a human kind.

People are the key to success in law firms. Having the right team to attract, develop, and retain these people is one of the most important roles in a firm. It cannot be measured in fee earning hours.

But what is the opportunity cost of not having these people specialists in place in your firm? Ensuring that you have the right human capital expertise to protect and grow your competitive advantage in a fast changing and disruptive market in the volatile, uncertain, complex, and ambiguous (VUCA) world that we all live and work in is a business-critical issue. Working in HR and talent management is an exciting and ever evolving career opportunity. An opportunity to be right at the heart of a law firm – its people.

References

1. Laura McNair, Totum Partners, www.totumpartners.com/.
2. See Chapter 12: The emerging world of ESG for more information.
3. www.cipd.co.uk/
4. www.cipd.co.uk/learn/training
5. https://peopleprofession.cipd.org/profession-map#gref
6. www.managers.org.uk/
7. www.changeboard.com/
8. www.mpfglobal.com/groups/people,-performance-culture.aspx
9. www.winmarkglobal.com/networks-chro/
10. www.cipd.co.uk/learn/events-networks/hr-leaders#gref
11. See CIPD career hub Career Transitions for a full account: www.cipd.co.uk/careers/career-guidance/career-transitions/rachel-brushfield.

Chapter 8:
Communications – bringing brand to life

By Hayley Geffin, head of communications, Mishcon de Reya

Introduction

As a teenager, I wanted to be a lawyer. My understanding of what that entailed was limited to television and film for quite some time, before I shadowed a criminal barrister for a week (with thanks to my friend's mother for making that connection). After that week, and through no fault of the barrister but mostly due to the sharp shock of the reality of criminal law, I decided not to pursue it and went on to read English at university.

However, while I lost interest in becoming a lawyer, I did not lose interest in the law. An avid follower of current affairs, it was obvious to me that law and lawyers were at the heart of business, politics, and social issues. Working with them meant access to a diverse range of disciplines – and I wanted that. My story is not a unique one. Law firms across the UK and the world are filled with smart, ambitious individuals who are not lawyers. It is common practice to call them non-lawyers. However, at my workplace, Mishcon de Reya LLP, where I began my career in communications more than 12 years ago, we call them business operations professionals.

The increasing centrality of business operations in my 12 years working in law cannot be overstated. The business has grown enormously in terms of headcount, revenue, and expansion into new markets in that time. This is a result of the commitment and belief that business operations is not "back office" or a necessary but rather lamentable cost center, but core to our success as a business. From cyber security experts to data scientists to people advisory teams to sales and marketing professionals, all of these and more add value to our proposition and, in many cases, to our bottom line.

In this chapter, I want to focus on the role of communications in law: the different opportunities available, the skills required for success, and how to build an effective and diverse team.

Your brand

Communications within law firms can span a huge range of disciplines and it varies hugely by organization in much the same way as marketing or business development. The truth is that all three work in service of one thing: brand. Brand, it perhaps goes without saying, is who you are. Everything feeds into it: your values and purpose, what you do, and how you do it.

The effective expression of your brand does not happen overnight. Nor does it happen through grand, singular initiatives or advertising campaigns alone. The expression of brand is brought to life every day in everything that you produce. Your brand should be alive in every piece of content on your website, every media comment, every internal announcement. The role for communications is to bring the brand to life.

In my years working in communications in the legal sector, it was not always thus. The primary role for communications in the 2000s was editorial – reviewing content with an expert eye for language. PR agencies bridged the gap with the media, social platforms were an oddity explored by tech and digital teams, and internal communications sought more to inform than to engage. Today, each of these disciplines – editorial, PR, and internal communications – are still critical, but the interplay between them is equally important and especially in times of such far-reaching change.

Editorial

Content is critical in the expression of your brand and should be cohesive in that expression. Responsibility for editorial means oversight of every piece of content your firm produces. It means that you and your team are editors in chief of your firm website and the articles written for it, your social media feeds, your pitch documents, your marketing collateral, and every event invitation or email alert that you send. Naturally, this requires an aptitude and command of language, as well as the ability to grasp complicated topics quickly and, where necessary, confidence in helping simplify them for your readership.

The beauty of the editorial role in a law firm is that it allows you to dive into an enormous range of subject matter. From untangling EU regulation from UK regulation post-Brexit to understanding NFTs, esports, or what happens to pets when couples divorce: a day of reviewing content is rarely the same.

Media relations/PR

When I began my career, to me at least, PR seemed a preserve of the glamorous – something that luxury brands or celebrities were engaged in, not businesses. I had a lot to learn! Having worked in the industry and with PR firm colleagues for some time, I now believe there is a core distinction to be made between media relations and PR.

Media relations is the management of your firm's media profile – this includes drafting press releases but is in no way limited to that. It requires working with your senior team and many lawyers to understand the core messages, building relationships with journalists and publications, and undertaking press briefings (on record and off record).

PR incorporates all of these but casts the net wider to include public affairs and lobbying. Law firms may have the capability for the latter but, since public affairs expertise is generally gained through experience of working in the political sphere, law firms generally engage external advisors for this.

Media relations is by its nature high stakes. In engaging with the media typically you are doing two things: seeking to promote your brand or seeking to protect it. In executing the former, you must never lose sight of the bigger picture, and the larger the firm is the more potential for legal or commercial conflict. The latter does not keep to regular hours and you need a cool head in counselling and supporting your team and your senior colleagues through crises.

Internal communications

In many larger businesses, the external and internal communications functions are separate. There is sound logic to this as the disciplines are quite different. However, keeping them entirely separate can jeopardize the opportunity to learn from each discipline, plus it can create a real disconnect between what you say to your people and what you say to the world. I have found that oversight of both disciplines is critical in building an effective strategy and that while some team members may focus more on one than another, as a whole the team is integrated and all the better for it.

As I mentioned earlier, internal communications c. 2010 was largely a one-way street; a broadcast arm that transmitted messages but did not make much space for two-way conversations. This has changed dramatically, particularly since the advent of the COVID-19 pandemic.

Your workforce are the greatest advocates you have. You can have the best content, thousands upon thousands of Twitter followers, and feature on the front page of newspapers, but if your people don't believe in, fight for, and embody your brand I'm afraid you're doomed.

To create a firm of advocates requires a huge investment of time and nurturing opportunities for two-way feedback and interaction. Understanding your audience is never more critical than when it's your own. To be skilled at internal communications requires you to take an interest in your colleagues and how they consume information. It requires a willingness to experiment with platforms and formats for communication – from written content to live events to podcasts and animation, no stone should be left unturned. It also requires you to advocate for your colleagues. Confidence and the ability to influence are critical.

Growing a team

It has often been said that law firms are distinct from other businesses. The partnership model, while it exists in other industries, is so important to the culture of law firms and if you haven't experienced that before it can take a little getting used to. However, much about training as a lawyer and progressing to partnership has not changed in decades. Generally, in the UK, lawyers specialize early and work in their chosen field for their whole career. Communications is different. It is, for want of a better term, industry agnostic. The skills one develops working in communications for banks, management consultancies, big brands like airlines and global manufacturers, small, agile comms agencies, and non-governmental organizations are not only transferable, they are desirable.

I have benefited enormously in my career through a simple principle passed on by my manager and mentor: don't restrict your influences to your own industry. Look to brands that inspire you and seek to learn from them. Apply some of their thinking to your own business – for example, at Mishcon de Reya back in 2010 we re-imagined our website taking inspiration from the biggest one in the world – Google. Allow your audience to have that same user-friendly, customer-focused approach: ask them what they are looking for. At the time, it was ground-breaking for a law firm to straight up ask: how can we help you? Our text box is still prominent on Mishcon.com today and we've noticed many other firms take inspiration from us since then.

This is also true in building a communications team. For example, communications professionals from large consumer FMCG (fast-moving consumer goods) brands understand brand like no other. They know how to connect with their audience and they have pursued creative ways to do this through content creation and savvy social media use. A law firm does not necessarily have the same kind of customer base as Apple or Coca Cola, but a lot of what these international juggernauts have unlocked is nonetheless transferable. Individuals coming from that background have so much to offer – provided your law firm is brave enough to experiment.

In a media crisis, who better by your side than someone who has worked in government positions or with national public organizations? The stories they will have been part of will have been the news issues of the day – the sort of event where the phone just does not stop ringing. They can share expertise on how to keep a cool head and are living proof that crises end, which can be extremely reassuring. These individuals also understand working with a vast range of stakeholders and can apply these principles to the sort of multi-level hierarchy you may find in a law firm.

To understand how to communicate organizational or structural change in an organization, who better than someone from the world of banking and finance? In the last ten years increased regulatory scrutiny has changed the very fabric of that industry. Internal communications professionals coming from banking and finance have an in-depth understanding about how large organizations separated into different disciplines react to change – they know what works in communicating with their people and what doesn't. This is gold dust.

For those moving into communications from another discipline or for people just starting out in their careers, there is just one thing you need above and beyond all the transferable skills from other roles or your education: curiosity. The best communications professionals are always curious. They ask a lot of questions and they want to understand the how and the why of any issue that comes their way. In a law firm, this means not bypassing an unfamiliar lexicon but taking the time to decode it and to decode it for others – clients and colleagues alike – with the content you create or oversee. It may have killed the cat, but in communications curiosity is only ever a positive!

The sky's the limit

The legal market is competitive. Its clients are demanding and exacting with complex needs and many options to choose from. For a law firm to stand out requires more than strategic and technical excellence from its lawyers – operational excellence is also critical. For clients to trust a law firm with their business they want to have confidence in how the law firm runs its own.

This requires commitment across the vast range of business operations from those that have been there since day one – finance and risk and compliance – to those that have developed more recently – ESG and impact.

What I love about communications is getting to work with colleagues across all these areas, helping them to articulate what they do, and working with them on the most serious issues they face. Since the COVID-19 pandemic, these bonds have only grown stronger. So, too, has law firms' management teams' confidence in and reliance on professionals from outside law to help run, promote, and protect their business.

Communications teams and roles vary, but a representative structure from most junior to senior may be communications apprentice, communications executive, social media executive, communications manager and head or director of communications, the latter reporting into the partnership and management board.

For me, having the opportunity to sit at the top table and strategize with my most senior colleagues on communicating the most critical issues to our internal and external stakeholders is a privilege. It is also evidence that not only is there space in law firms for ambitious people who are not lawyers, but that the sky is the limit.

Chapter 9: Oh the places you'll go: careers in legal innovation

By Amy Monaghan, director of client innovation, Perkins Coie

Introduction

My career path is far from ordinary, particularly for a lawyer. But it has set me up well for a career in legal innovation. In this chapter I'll draw links from my unique path to my everyday work as a legal innovator. I'll provide an overview of the different areas of legal that my role touches and how my team and I engage in cross-functional collaboration to promote change. Lastly, I'll discuss the types of skills and roles that are being created (some by me) to meet innovation opportunities. To note, my experience is largely informed by my roles in mid-size and large law firms primarily serving the corporate sector.

To start, I think some background and context on innovation in the legal industry is needed so I plan to briefly cover this topic. The term "legal innovation" covers a broad spectrum of opportunities including emerging areas of law, innovation of laws and their interpretation, innovation in the way that lawyers work on matters and issues, and innovation in the delivery of legal services. Where I focus my talents is innovating the business of law and how law firms provide legal services to clients. This work requires innovation professionals that have multi-disciplinary skills, including legal experience, as well as business expertise. The current majority of opportunities lies within innovation of the delivery of legal services.

My path to my role

On paper, I was a very unlikely law school candidate. I have a background in fine art and undergraduate education in visual and critical studies. When I first started articulating that I wanted to attend law school, I was met with a nearly universal question of "what kind of lawyer" I wanted to be. And my slightly snarky response was almost universally "a different kind!". My reasoning for wanting to pursue law was informed by a few different experiences.

First, I became very interested in cultural property issues; things like provenance, property rights related to artwork, insurance-related issues, and the institutional frameworks of museums, galleries, and auction houses. I decided to focus on this topic for my thesis work and quickly narrowed in on a subtopic of art theft. Through my research I discovered a new potential path of merging my art interests and experience with a law degree to potentially work with a law enforcement agency investigating crimes that involve cultural property. I learned that the FBI had a dedicated art crime team, and I was very interested in that as a potential career.[1] I had also been working as a freelance "portfolio manager" for several professional artists in Chicago during this time. This work involved digitizing artist portfolios so they could establish websites and send images of their work in digital format to galleries, collectors, and municipalities with public art programs. I also taught myself how to write grants, request for proposal responses, and website content. And there was a fair amount of event planning and relationship management skills that I developed doing this work.

Each of these experiences opened my eyes to the business side of art and it was more interesting to me as a career than being an artist. So, I endeavored to law school and found that I was interested in everything – except being a "traditional" lawyer. The best piece of advice I received prior to starting law school was to take as many courses as I could that would expose me to different ideas and concepts and not to worry about the bar exam (too much). I took this advice and explored as many topics as I could, eventually narrowing in on intellectual property and cultural property issues.

In my search to find a career that combined my creativity, technical curiosity, and business strategy interests, I tried on a few different "flavors" of roles. Along the way I acquired some key technical and non-technical skills that have proven immensely beneficial in my innovation roles:

- Software development concepts;
- How relational databases work and information architecture in general;
- Understanding how machine learning works, how to successfully train AI models and use them in the practice of law;
- Learning how to implement and manage technology platforms that attorneys and clients rely on;
- Learning how to listen to clients to understand what they are asking law firms to do;

- Basic project management skills;
- Design Thinking[2] methodologies; and
- Questioning the status quo (not so much a skill as a character trait) and adaptability to shifting landscapes and priorities.

Leading innovation in a law firm

So, what exactly is it that I do? The short answer is, I find ways to create or change how my firm delivers legal services so that we are consistently meeting evolving client needs. It's a broad mandate and my role touches many areas of the firm. What I focus on is largely influenced by internal and external forces that are driving, or at least underlining, innovation in the industry. It's important in this line of work to analyze the ever-changing ecosystem because these forces will ultimately influence the changes my organization will need to implement, and where possible, be a driver of some of the forces in the industry.[3]

Since I spend the majority of my time working on innovation of service delivery models, I thought it would be helpful to outline the various areas of legal and law firm business that my role touches/collaborates with/oversees.

Technology

My team and I are solutions creators, so we incorporate a lot of technology tools into our toolkit. We design and architect solutions based on opportunities uncovered through our engagement with clients. A lot of our solutions are built using third party software that we can customize, configure, and integrate with other solutions in order to create "total" solutions where possible. We also engage with in-house and external developers and other software professionals as needed when "out-of-the-box" software doesn't meet our needs. Our toolkit is quite expansive, and we are constantly evaluating new technology in order to stay on top of best in breed offerings. One of the skills I look for in potential team members is the ability to quickly master new technologies and understand the fundamentals of software development. Even though we aren't software engineers, we need to be able to understand the abilities, and limits, of technology tools, how they interoperate, and how to collaborate with developers.

Product and process design

Solution creation is product design, particularly when we are building custom solutions from the ground up. Many considerations beyond technical functionality go into product design – supportability, scalability, direct and indirect costs, anticipated ROI, and potential target market and marketability, to name a few. Since we operate within a law firm, and not a software shop, these can sometimes be challenging considerations for a variety of reasons so product design and development must be approached strategically to ensure resources are deployed where they will have the most impact.

Underlying all solution development is process design. In order to solve problems, we must understand the current state, and since we are in a services industry, everything has a process. Most, if not all, of the solutions we create include process design or optimization as a critical component.

Business model development

Most innovation requires brand-new business models or changes to existing ones. Because my function is designing the innovation to be implemented, we are closely involved with developing the accompanying business models that will support innovation. This is a cross-functional effort with other operational leaders at our firm. As an example, we have developed a suite of products that compliment a certain area of practice. We are offering creative pricing options for bundled legal services combined with access to our technology solutions. Since this is a new offering from the firm, we worked with operational leaders from our finance, pricing, marketing, and technology groups to develop business models that will help us sell and support these new services.

Pricing

Quantifying the value of innovation is a fun puzzle! The solutions we create are fundamentally shifting the traditional legal services model because we are not purely translating hours into revenue. We work closely with our pricing professionals to align how we price our innovative offerings with the firm's overall pricing and profitability strategy and goals.

Legal project management

We work closely with our legal project managers, particularly when we are implementing new solutions to clients and practices. At Perkins Coie, legal project managers work directly with our clients to define and manage scope of work, manage and monitor budgets, and identify opportunities for improvement during the work cycles. Because our legal project managers have a broad lens into our clients' needs, they are ideal partners for identifying and implementing innovative solutions, particularly as they improve and optimize legal work and the delivery of legal services.

Marketing

Similar to pricing, articulating the value of innovation in a way that resonates with our clients is an artform in itself. We partner with our marketing professionals to find ways to communicate what value our solutions offer and how they meet the needs of our clients. Internal communications and marketing plans are of equal importance to our client-facing ones for a few reasons. First, our attorneys interface with our clients on a more regular basis than we do so educating them on what innovative offerings we have is important information they can pass on to clients in opportune moments. Second, it helps us promote a culture of innovation by highlighting new ideas and efforts we are trying. Lastly, is also helps surface new ideas and connect dots that we may not have direct sightline into, but our attorneys do. Quite often, after presenting internally to a practice group or legal team on an innovative offering that we are rolling out for a different segment, partners will reach out and ask for collateral they can include in pitches for new work. They may not see a direct connection to existing work but can see a connection that will help win potential work.

Leadership

A key part of my role is leading teams, committees, and projects/initiatives. There are numerous excellent resources readily available on leadership that are worthy of your time, so I won't dive deep into the different methodologies and philosophies here.[4] I think it's worth briefly discussing how important relationships are in this line of work. Innovation, at its core, is change. And change is difficult for everyone, even when we want change to occur. I have found it immensely beneficial to spend time developing and nourishing relationships with people that I work with to ensure that we are aligned in our ambitions and understand the job to be done.[5] Relationship building is an often overlooked aspect of innovation leadership but it is, in my opinion, the most important role because change requires political, emotional, and physical willingness and you will be hard pressed to implement change without trusting relationships with the people who will experience the changes.

Strategy

Innovation is a critical business function for any organization with ambitions to grow. As we saw with the COVID-19 pandemic, it is also a critical function for organizations to adapt to changing landscapes.[6] Because resources are finite, having an innovation strategy to inform where an organization should deploy its innovation resources and talent is critical. I have experienced this firsthand and have found it necessary to be involved in the strategy-setting process so that I can align our innovation goals with the goals of the firm. Without this alignment, we risk investing in the wrong areas and wasting precious time and money. Innovation is an inherently risk-taking activity because you are making bets on the future. Best not to go at it blindly but rather spend time understanding strategic aims to guide your innovation activities.

New and emerging roles in legal innovation

As you can see, this work is quite varied and collaborative and requires a broad range of skills and expertise. It's been interesting to watch new roles emerge in the growing field of legal innovation and I will close this chapter with some examples of opportunities that are opening up for professionals.

- Innovation leaders. We've seen an increase in innovation leadership opportunities and there's a broad range of levels, from chief innovation officers, directors of innovation, and varying levels of innovation managers. These roles have broad mandates that are tailored to each organization's strategic aims. Generally, people in these roles are responsible for setting innovation strategy, managing teams who execute strategic projects, and educating their organization on innovation opportunities.
- Product designers.[7] A growing proportion of innovation functions within legal involve product development. This is an interesting area because it's not traditional product development but shares some characteristics. More often than not, product and solution designers are finding ways to leverage multiple "off the shelf" solutions to create an end-to-end product to meet the needs of end customers. The skillset to do this successfully requires technical expertise and substantive knowledge of the practice of law.
- Product managers. Similar to product designers, legal product managers are in growing demand. These roles manage the roadmaps for innovation solutions and serve as the voice of customers (both clients and internal attorneys). This type of role liaises with technical and subject matter expert teams as well as operational leaders within firms to ensure that products continue to meet needs by improving existing functionality and expanding to new use cases.
- Relationship specialists. As previously discussed, this work hinges on trusting relationships with clients, strategic partners, internal and

external stakeholders, and firm leadership. This type of engagement goes beyond traditional client relationship management and is a role I anticipate becoming more in demand in the near future.

My team incorporates aspects of each of these roles and we all wear many different hats, which makes the work all the more interesting. We operate iteratively and as agile as possible in order to meet opportunities as they emerge. This type of nimbleness is critical to innovation work but can be challenging in complex organizations with competing demands. This is part of what makes the work so interesting and engaging, for people who are up for the challenge.

Conclusion

It's a very exciting time in the legal industry because there are many opportunities for innovation. There are numerous problems with potential scalable solutions across the industry that will require many more innovators with creativity and business acumen to solve. As you hopefully have discerned, there is no one path to a legal innovation career. There are many possible entry points for anyone interested in this type of career, which can be appealing for people interested in legal but put off by law school and the post-qualification requirements of a legal degree. It's not an easy role – change is difficult and leading change within large organizations with hundreds of years of history and culture is doubly challenging. It is, however, always exciting, intriguing, and in my experience, a lot more fun!

References

1. See www.fbi.gov/investigate/violent-crime/art-theft.
2. See www.ideou.com/blogs/inspiration/what-is-design-thinking; see also https://dschool.stanford.edu/resources/design-thinking-bootleg.
3. See www.legalevolution.org/2021/11/legal-evolution-is-industrial-evolution-277/.
4. Adam Grant, John P. Kotter, Kim Scott, Brene Brown, and Simon Sinek are personal favorites in this genre.
5. See https://hbr.org/2016/09/know-your-customers-jobs-to-be-done.
6. See www.mckinsey.com/business-functions/strategy-and-corporate-finance/our-insights/innovation-in-a-crisis-why-it-is-more-critical-than-ever.
7. See www.legalevolution.org/2021/11/legal-evolution-is-industrial-evolution-277/ "To create scalable practices, we should move more experiences from services, to operations, to products. This approach can create far more value from limited subject matter expertise for a broader range of clients and customers." See also

https://hbr.org/2016/09/putting-products-into-services "In the same way that product companies build innovation units to incubate ideas, services companies should set up teams devoted to developing products internally. It's important to make such a team somewhat autonomous; it needs its own budget, people, goals, and metrics. But keep it connected to the business units, since that's where product ideas will arise. Create a two-way exchange in which business units can come to the product team with ideas – and vice versa – while you empower the team to incubate those ideas."

Chapter 10:

Legal operations – transforming the way legal services are delivered

By Tammy Heydenrych, managing consultant, and Tom Evans, legal operations consultant, Norton Rose Fulbright

Solving the challenge of legal's value gap

A staggering 75 percent of CEOs don't believe that their legal function delivers sufficient value to justify the time and money spent.[1] This clearly signals a stark gap between the value that in-house legal teams (and by extension the law firms that support them) think they deliver to their business customers, and what those business customers perceive that value to be. How then do GCs and law firms close this gap?

The first challenge is defining what value means to legal teams and their business customers. Shifting the perception of in-house legal as a cost center to a value provider requires strategic business partnering, relationship building, and the use of data to objectively measure performance and not simply activities.

In an increasingly uncertain and volatile environment where the risks posed to business are becoming more complex, and the potential impact more severe, many legal teams find themselves in "firefighting mode", so busy dealing with day-to-day challenges that longer-term strategic planning and implementation becomes a side-of-desk task.

Notwithstanding that 98 percent of GCs acknowledge that transformation is critical to their success, less than a third are implementing strategies to achieve this transformation.[2]

Many lawyers therefore seek specialist legal operations support, suggesting that they lack these specialist skills, and/or have limited time, resources, or appetite to formulate appropriate strategies and, critically, to successfully implement those strategies and embed change within their teams.

Bridging this gap is the role of legal operations.

So, what is legal operations?

If you asked ten GCs to define the meaning of legal operations, you would likely get ten different answers. To some, legal operations is synonymous with technology, data, or artificial intelligence. To others it means process improvement and standardization, or external resource management.

Broadly speaking, legal operations encompasses everything related to delivery of legal services that is outside of the legal advice itself. To put it another way, traditional legal services focus on the *what* – namely the advice itself. Legal operations looks at *how*, *why*, *when*, *where*, and by *whom* this legal advice is delivered.

In practice, this makes for an incredibly broad legal operations landscape. Legal professionals must navigate a myriad of sub-specialisms, from strategy, resourcing, and financial management to knowledge management, legal design, technology, and data analytics – to name a few!

This chapter explores the growth of legal operations, how this has influenced existing and emerging careers in law, and the skills required of those interested in a career in legal operations.

The growth of legal operations

Although the concept of *"legal operations as a career"* is more prevalent today than it was even five years ago, it is still very much in its infancy relative to other disciplines. This is not surprising given that the legal profession has historically been slow to embrace change. However, events such as the financial crisis of 2008 and the COVID-19 pandemic have forced even the most reluctant lawyers to embrace new ways of working (and thinking!) to reduce costs, improve efficiencies and service delivery, support innovation, and enable remote working.

Additionally, trends have emerged that have influenced, and will continue to influence, the growth of legal operations and related career paths. Some of these key trends are explored in more detail below.

Running the legal function like a business – from cost center to strategic business partner and enabler

Unlike a sales function, which looks to generate revenue and ultimately profit for the business, a legal function's value has historically been seen as the mitigation of risk or "keeping the lights on" from a legal perspective, rather than as business enablers. Mounting financial pressures mean legal teams are increasingly asked to do more for less, placing the focus on costs rather than strategic value creation. The consequence of viewing legal teams through this lens is that it often limits the levers a GC can pull to contribute to the financial success of the business. In practice, this is means either headcount reduction or budget cuts, including for example seeking the lowest possible external counsel rates.

Whilst the commercial realities – particularly post-pandemic – cannot be ignored, strategic business partnering is more important than ever as legal teams and their external legal advisors navigate increasing levels of risk and guide their organizations and clients through unchartered territories. Ultimately, the challenge in-house legal departments face is that they don't control demand for legal services but are held accountable for the costs related to that demand. Simply cutting costs or reducing headcount without fully understanding the anticipated demand is a recipe for disaster. This is compounded by the fact that many lawyers are not trained or equipped to take on these multidisciplinary roles, raising the question: *"What is the role of the modern lawyer?"*

An attempt to answer this question has led to the development of models such as the T-Shaped Lawyer,[3] O-Shaped Lawyer,[4] the Delta Model,[5] and the Bionic Lawyer.[6] Each model offers a perspective of the skills the modern lawyer needs. Ultimately, what they all have in common is the proposition that lawyers today need to be multi-skilled business and strategic advisors, with capabilities beyond technical legal advice and risk management.

Pursuing this line of thinking, there is the potential for legal to be seen as a profit driver. This is in fact already occurring across functions with more mature legal operations capabilities and embedded data strategies. For example, providing horizon scanning for regulatory changes can offer a significant competitive advantage to the wider business, informing new product launches, or other strategic growth initiatives. On an operational level, being able to provide key insights into an organization's contracts can help inform strategic revenue generation as well as cost avoidance decisions.

Expanding dedicated legal operations roles

In 2021, 40 percent of organizations registered an increase in the number of dedicated legal operations staff employed, building on the same percentage increase reported in 2020.[7] Looking forward, Gartner predicts that by 2024, legal departments will replace 20 percent of generalist lawyers with non-lawyer staff.[8] This view is shared by KPMG, which predicts that a legal chief operations officer will be just as important as a GC by 2025.[9]

This presents an exciting opportunity for those looking to move from a traditional legal role or other industry into legal operations. We are already seeing evidence of this expansion of legal operations capabilities, with 40 percent of legal functions reporting having a non-lawyer in the role of legal operations manager (or equivalent) in 2020, compared to only 20 percent in 2018.[10]

The focus on how legal services are delivered and the use of technology as an enabler

In the introduction to this chapter, we spoke about the way that legal services are delivered – the *how*. This is reflective of a much broader focus across the legal industry on service delivery, both from the perspective of law firms serving their external clients as well as in-house legal teams delivering to their internal clients. It is no longer sufficient to simply deliver technically correct legal advice (everyone professes to do this!). The way in which it is delivered is now a key focus area for any forward-looking legal services provider seeking to differentiate themselves in a competitive market.

In 2005, Bain & Co highlighted a "delivery gap" between companies and their customers. Whilst 80 percent of companies believed they delivered outstanding value and superior customer service, only eight percent of their customers agreed.[11] Much has changed since 2005, but in a legal industry that can often be slow to adapt, it is difficult to argue that a such a delivery gap is not still present to some extent today.

A spotlight on this has resulted in a slow but clear shift in the way we look at many aspects of legal work. Advice can now be delivered via interactive portals rather than via email. Law firm services are increasingly delivered through alternative fee arrangements or using value-based billing, rather than hourly rates. Sales teams that value speed to market can use questionnaires to generate contracts and eSignature software to facilitate what was previously a cumbersome closing process, enabling self-service and freeing up lawyers to focus on higher value tasks. Legal departments can manage their workloads using specialized legal front doors and matter-management technology, rather than their email inbox.

You will note that much of this focuses on the *experience* of delivering legal services, rather than the services themselves, whilst using technology as an enabler to support people and processes. In fact, Gartner predicts legal technology spending will increase to approximately 12 percent of in-house budgets by 2025, a threefold increase from 2020 levels.[12] Legal teams will need to think carefully about how to develop their technology roadmaps and manage the implementation of new technology tools.

These new ways of working are no doubt a step-change from the way things have been traditionally done by most in-house teams and law firms. With lawyers rightly devoting a great deal of their energy and expertise to the *what* (providing expert legal and risk management advice), there is a growing need for both generalist and specialist legal operations professionals to drive the change in the way services are delivered.

Legal operations taxonomy

Influenced by these trends, the legal operations landscape, and, by extension, the scope of legal operations roles will continue to evolve to meet market demand.

There exist various models designed to capture this landscape and reflect the various processes, specialties, and interdependencies that characterize legal operations today. One such example is depicted below.

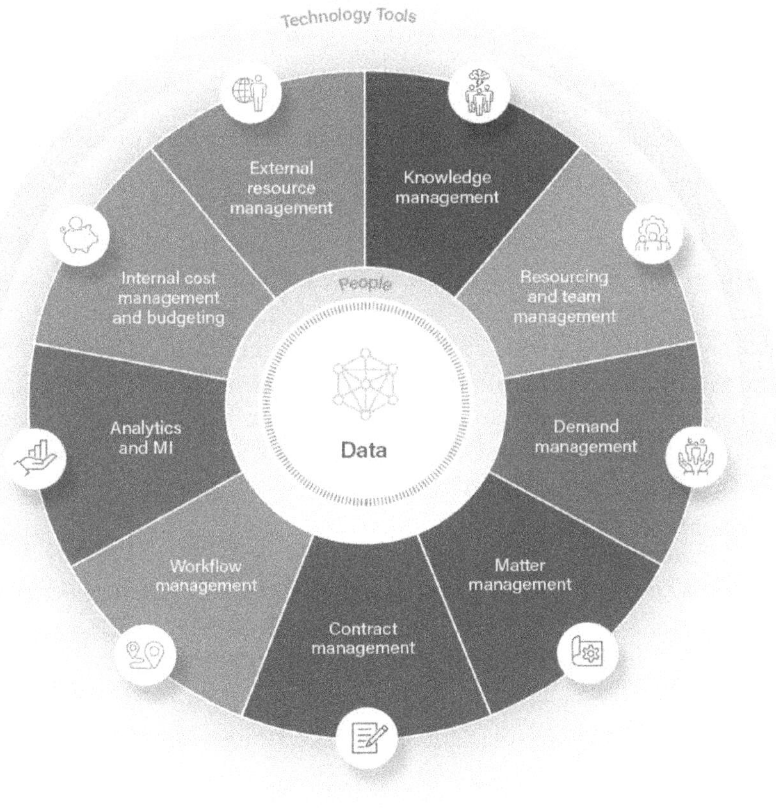

NRF Transform Legal Operations Consulting Process Taxonomy © 2022

This legal operations taxonomy attempts to codify the framework, language, and concepts used to categorize key legal operations processes and can be a useful starting point to identify the legal operations roles and skills that are emerging in the industry. It is not static, however, and will continue to evolve as will the role of legal operations professionals.

Each of the dimensions or spokes of the wheel comprises strategic elements (planning and prioritization) and operational elements (analysis, design, and implementation). These are underpinned by the use of data that should inform the design of effective strategies, frameworks, and processes, whilst ensuring the right people are in place with the right skills. The outer ring of the wheel reflects the use of technology as an enabler to improve or support those strategies, processes, and people.

So, what opportunities does this provide for a legal operations professional?

As is evident from the above taxonomy, there are several specialties to be explored. We discuss some of these below.

Legal project management

We are seeing a growing appreciation of the importance of using legal project managers to manage complex litigation matters or mergers and acquisitions. Not only does this free up lawyers' time to focus on the legal work, but it improves the scoping of matters, controls costs, supports more appropriate resource allocation, and improves outcomes.

It is no wonder then that in-house legal teams are increasingly expecting their law firms to provide LPM resources to improve service delivery and are looking to expand their in-house capability as well.

The role of the LPM is to manage all or most of the operational aspects of a matter (i.e., anything that is not legal advice). Some of the activities that this might include would be:

Project planning

- Project managers spend time at the outset of the matter setting up a project plan, which looks to forecast all foreseeable elements of the project such as scope, timelines, resourcing, budget, and risks.
- This is in contrast to many legal matters that often start at short notice, with little thought given to timelines and budget until the wheels are already in motion.

Risk management

- Whereas lawyers focus on legal risk, legal project managers focus on operational risks at the matter level.
- A good legal project manager will keep an ongoing log of risks throughout the matter lifecycle and have a plan in place for mitigating each of these along with how to respond should the risk materialize.
- Good risk management cannot be undervalued and, combined with a project plan, can offer significant savings when issues do arise during the life of a matter as outlined above.

Matter coordination

- As well as setting up a project plan, it is of course vitally important for a project manager to be able to ensure everybody sticks to the plan (as much as possible). Legal project managers therefore should be adept at ensuring multiple work streams run as smoothly as possible from a scope, timeline, and budget perspective. Where scope changes, it is up to the project manager to relay the effect of this to stakeholders and propose solutions and alternatives that work.

Whilst many legal project managers move into the role from an alternative project management background, this is certainly not a prerequisite to the role. Given that some of the most important skills for a legal project manager are matter coordination, financial management, and stakeholder management, it is possible to transition into an LPM role from, say, a transaction management role, a finance role, or a legal secretarial role. The key factor is demonstrating an ability to take on some of the responsibilities outlined above.

The fundamentals of legal project management draw heavily on traditional project management, although with legal nuances. Therefore, candidates with experience in project management from other fields (e.g., oil and gas, finance) would be well-placed to take a step into legal project management. Additionally, lawyers with some experience and/or training in project management can leverage their combination of skills to transition into such a role.

External resource management

External legal spend is estimated to account for over 58 percent of all in-house legal spend.[13] As such, effectively managing that spend can be a highly effective driver in reducing overall budget. Furthermore, many in-house teams are unable to clearly articulate to the wider business how well their panel firms are performing against business objectives. It is therefore no surprise that external resource management continues to develop as an important discipline within legal operations.

External resource management often (but not always) focuses on either one or both of the following areas, each requiring a unique set of skills.

Panel management

- Although favored by organizations with large volumes of work, or those requiring specialist legal support, the creation of a panel offers a number of benefits to both in-house teams and law firms. For in-house teams it enables better commercial terms and improved service delivery, and for law firms it can mean a larger share of wallet and stronger client relationships – if done well, a win-win situation.
- A legal operations professional working in this space will be focused on maximizing the value from their panel, whilst maintaining a positive relationship with panel firms. Rather than pushing firms into a "race to the bottom" on rates, they should focus on developing a sustainable panel model, allowing the *right work* to be done at the *right price* by the *right people* at the *right firm*. This requires a smart segmentation of matter types, effective use of data, being in a position to compare like to like through objective scoring criteria, and ongoing management of firm performance.

Tender management

Whilst a panel will govern the overall relationship with law firms at a high level, there is much that can be done on a matter-by-matter basis. A legal operations professional in this space will be asking the following questions and identifying the answers that can help the business derive the most value:

- Which firms are best suited to take part in the tender?
- What should the scope of the work be (often considered in conjunction with legal project managers above)?
- How can this matter be most efficiently delivered?
- What seniority of lawyer is needed for this matter?
- What is the most suitable fee structure?
- How should we assess and compare law firms?

In many cases, the legal function may not have a panel or a tender process, in which case the requirements might be to set up a panel or design and implement a tender process.

Candidates with procurement experience or those who have worked in business development, commercial management, or on bids for example, would likely have transferrable skills that could be useful in this context.

Technology selection and implementation

With increased focus on efficiency and service delivery, it is almost impossible to work in legal and not come across the term "legal technology". It can be tempting to jump to the selection and implementation of the latest technology tool as a quick fix before fully understanding the problem.

The challenge, given the sheer volume of technology on the market, is knowing where to start. However, the selection, implementation, and maintenance of technology is a far cry from the day-to-day of a typical lawyer and requires a very different skillset and knowledge-base. Whilst lawyers should certainly be across their legal tech, they should also know when to bring in specialist skills needed to select, implement, and manage this legal tech.

In practice, this might include:

- Condensing a large amount of disparate information, pain points, aspirations, and questions into a clear set of requirements that can be understood by technology vendors and consultants.
- Demonstrating the right level of market knowledge to know which vendors to consider, what questions to ask, and to speak in their language.
- An ability to manage multiple stakeholders frequently speaking in different terms with competing priorities. Legal is very often at the back of the queue when it comes to IT support, for example, but will be heavily reliant on their engagement for success.
- Planning and managing change, building consensus, and articulating the benefits to secure buy-in and ensure the tool and associated processes and ways of working are embedded.

Building your legal operations career

Whilst there are currently few formal, accredited academic qualifications that cover the full breadth of the legal operations landscape, this should not be seen as a barrier to securing a role in legal operations. In fact, most recruiters recognize this and instead tend to focus on candidates with experience across one or more legal operations specialties (for example, process improvement, panel management, technology tools, or business operating model design). Knowledge of the legal industry is highly advantageous but it is also not uncommon to see candidates with operations, procurement, data analytics, or technology experience transitioning from other industries.

If you are currently in a legal role, whether in-house or within a law firm, look for opportunities for innovation and improvement within your team or function. Offer to participate in or lead improvement projects, even if as a side-of-desk initiative. These initiatives do not always require significant investment in time or resources. Start small, fail forward, and iterate! This will help you develop your skillset, raise your profile internally, and build experience for your CV. These projects could include mapping your current processes to identify inefficiencies, considering ways to improve the allocation of legal work within teams, improving internal reporting and data analytics capabilities, rolling out a new piece of technology, or even creating playbooks to simplify your contracting process. Use this as an opportunity to build your cross-functional network and seek advice and input from other teams such as IT, operations or resource management.

Your organization may have internal training or be willing to fund external training to help you build transferable skills such as project management, lean or agile methodologies, financial acumen, legal design, data analytics, or change management. All of these skills are key components in the toolkit of a well-rounded legal operations professional.

Depending on where you are in your career, you may also want to consider a graduate scheme. Places on such schemes are highly competitive, but candidates from a variety of different backgrounds have the opportunity to gain exposure across a breadth of business and legal operations topics. Norton Rose Fulbright LLP, for example, runs one such graduate scheme[14] within NRF Transform, the firm's innovation change program. The scheme enables candidates to rotate across various specialties, providing practical, hands-on experience, and the opportunity to move into permanent roles in teams such as legal operations consulting, applied technology, legal design, or innovation upon completing the scheme.

Learning comes in many forms. Formal education, on-the-job learning, or graduate schemes are not the only way to upskill and build your network. There is a plethora of free online content, industry events, and communities. Joining the CLOC[15] network, for example, would give you access to seminars, thought leadership content, templates, advice, and networking events. Law firms and consultants are also increasingly offering insights and opportunities to network with other industry professionals to help guide lawyers embarking on a journey into legal operations.

Mindset over skillset

Given the evolving and broad nature of legal operations roles, there is no "correct" approach to carving out a niche for yourself. What is important however, is your *mindset.*

As highlighted in this chapter, there is a diverse range of discrete, but interconnected, disciplines across which a legal operations professional can add value. The skills required for each of these are equally diverse, which can make it difficult to know where to start, or indeed how to develop your career.

Ultimately, legal operations is about improving the way that things are done. Therefore, rather than purely focusing on technical skillsets, a continuous improvement or growth mindset, adaptability, curiosity, being comfortable with ambiguity, and being a creative problem-solver will provide you with a strong foundation for success.

References

1. General Counsel Roundtable & Plexus Thought Leaders Research: https://go.legalgateway.co/rs/083-ZLK-944/images/The Legal Transformation Playbook %28slide deck%29.pdf.
2. *Ibid.*
3. The T Shaped Lawyer: www.legalbusinessworld.com/post/2017/12/22/the-t-shaped-lawyer.
4. O Shaped Lawyer: www.oshapedlawyer.com/overview.
5. Natalie Runyon and Alyson Carrel, *Adapting for 21st Century Success: The Delta Competency Model*, Thomson Reuters, 2019.
6. www.inhouselawyer.co.uk/feature/a-call-to-arms-for-the-bionic-lawyer/
7. 2021 State of the Industry Survey, Corporate Legal Operations Consortium.
8. Five Legal Technology Trends Changing In-House Legal Departments: www.gartner.com/smarterwithgartner/5-legal-technology-trends-changing-in-house-legal-departments.
9. Ten predictions: the legal function in 2025 - KPMG Global: https://home.kpmg/xx/en/home/insights/2020/12/future-of-legal-article-series.html.
10. *State of the Legal Function*, Gartner, Inc., 2020.
11. *Closing the delivery gap*, Bain and Company, 2005.
12. www.gartner.com/en/newsroom/press-releases/2020-02-10-gartner-predicts-legal-technology-budgets-will-increase-threefold-by-2025

13. The GC350: Benchmarking Study for the In-House Community.
14. Business and legal operations graduate scheme, Norton Rose Fulbright: www.nortonrosefulbright.com/en-gb/careers/graduates/business-and-legal-operations-graduate-scheme.
15. https://cloc.org/

Chapter 11: The role of legal engineers

By Nina Gramcko, lawyer and manager, PwC Legal Germany

Competitive and commercial pressures, as well as client demand, are requiring law firms to find new and innovative ways to provide their legal services. As a result, new roles are emerging to ensure the excellence of the legal services offering: one of these is the legal engineer.

The term "legal engineering" has been used in different contexts for several decades. In the context of international law, it refers to the innovative creation of new legislation or legal orders, e.g., structuring extra-jurisdictional legal concepts under national law.[1] In addition, it has been used to describe the process of finding creative ways to apply existing legislation and regulations in banking law[2] and, more recently, how to apply existing or create new legislation in the new legal area of smart contracts, based on blockchain technology.[3]

Most recently, the term has been extended to describe the field of developing new and innovative ways to provide legal services, often in the context of legal technology (lawtech). Legal engineers can be found in start-ups, legal engineering law firms,[4] in-house legal departments, and traditional law firms.

There are different views of who a legal engineer is and what this role includes. These range from people who have an engineering background and build lawtech without necessarily having any legal training or in-depth legal knowledge, to trained and practicing lawyers with a passion for technology. The common denominator these views agree on is that in their role, legal engineers operate at the intersection between law and technology. Because of the importance of people and processes in the merger of law and technology, I would like to extend that and suggest that a legal engineer operates at the intersection of law, people, technology, and processes.

This chapter focuses on the role of legal engineers in law firms and covers what legal engineers do, what skills they should have, and – from a law firm's perspective – whether this role should be created and what law firms need to implement this role successfully.

What do legal engineers do?

The broadness and merit of the role greatly depend on the law firm's commercial, innovative, and operational set-up and strategy – which are frequently indicated by the size of the law firm – and whether complementing roles, e.g., legal service process manager, exist.

At this current lawtech adaptation stage, most law firms are more likely to implement commoditized, out-of-the-box lawtech products based on mature technology. The more innovatively evolved firms with a larger scale innovation set-up, distinct legal operations or innovation teams, and bigger budgets (typically larger firms) may include the deployment of customized and tailored technological solutions. Only the most evolved include novel and disruptive technology and have reached a more developed adaptation stage.

Hence, the focus and tasks of legal engineers in law firms include legal service process analysis and improvement (as an underlying necessity and stand-alone task), the implementation and application of procured technology, the deployment of customized technology, and related innovation projects.

It is at the core of a legal engineer's role to bring law, people, technology, and processes together to enhance the legal service offering and increase efficiencies. Legal engineers translate the needs of legal professionals into technological requirements in order to implement the most effective and efficient technology and processes. In their work, legal engineers greatly depend on the input and support of all those involved in providing legal services, i.e., the users of their implementations and processes. Therefore, legal engineers work closely with partners, fee earners, paralegals, service professionals, and the IT department for a successful implementation of lawtech that fits into the firm's IT infrastructure and innovation strategy.

Legal service process analysis and improvement

The basis of any implementation or deployment of lawtech should be a legal service process analysis. The legal engineer will – with the help of the process participants – analyze how a legal service is currently provided in order to identify bottlenecks, pain points, and redundant tasks.

Based on this analysis the legal engineer will then propose efficiency enhancing process adjustments and suggest the implementation of lawtech where appropriate.

An approved process model then forms the basis for a lawtech implementation.

Implementation of procured technology

Implementation of procured technology refers to the process of procuring and integrating lawtech products into the law firm's legal service processes and IT infrastructure, as well as the application of previously procured or bespoke technology to client work, e.g., document automation.

Selecting suitable lawtech for each use case and need is crucial. The variety of available lawtech products contributes to the expectation gap, which, according to the Law Society's 2019 Lawtech Adoption Research Report, exists "*between what law firms perceive can be delivered by the technologies and the reality of training and deploying these solutions for live client work*".[5] Legal engineers know the current state of technology as well as the legal service processes and needs and thus are able to help close this gap, actively managing expectations by acting out their intersectional role and involving the stakeholders and future users into the implementation process early on and communicating the possibilities and limitations of lawtech.

In parallel with the legal process analysis, the legal engineer must identify clear and specific functional and non-functional requirements for any lawtech to be implemented. This is done with input from users and other stakeholders who best understand their field, needs and (underlying) interests; e.g., which task(s) the lawtech should support, what their main pain points are, acceptance criteria, and potential Return on Investment (RoI).

Subsequently, the legal engineer will contact lawtech vendors and shortlist suitable products to present to stakeholders. In most cases, a pilot is set up to test one or two of these products on a small scale, allowing future users, stakeholders, and the project sponsor to provide their feedback. To accurately evaluate all relevant functionality, it is advisable to test with real data and documents. Once the pilot phase has concluded, stakeholders will consider the legal engineer's analysis of the pilot results and decide whether to move forwards with a full implementation or instead evaluate other products.

If a decision is made to move forwards and the lawtech is implemented, the legal engineer will introduce the lawtech and adjusted legal process(es). They will write user manuals, conduct training, and help the users to make sure the process runs smoothly, before it is deployed for live client work.

Throughout the implementation process, the intersectional role of legal engineers brings stakeholders, users, and the IT department together and makes sure the lawtech fits into the IT infrastructure of the firm, fulfilling the users' needs.

The more and earlier users and stakeholders are involved in the implementation process, the more they will own the result, achieving greater user acceptance and adoption.

Deployment of customized technology

The deployment of customized technology is typically considered when existing technology does not meet the identified requirements, or available lawtech is thought to be too inflexible to integrate with the firm's systems and processes, either now or in the future.

The role of the legal engineer in creating and deploying bespoke technology is one of a project manager and/or product owner, making sure the software requirements are understood by the engineers and the application is built accordingly. For business and complexity reasons, most law firms do not have an in-house software-engineering team, instead choosing to outsource product development.

Despite the benefits of customization, many law firms still shy away from bespoke solutions due to higher costs and execution risks. This might change with the increasing maturity of low-code and no-code technology, which allows citizen developers to create customized applications without needing to know how to code – a very exciting development for any legal engineer.

Innovation projects

Beyond the topics already discussed, additional innovation projects are often used to promote the work of legal engineers within the firm. These projects aim to enhance the firm's innovation mindset and change processes by increasing the awareness of lawtech and its role in delivering efficient legal services. This work is often closely linked to the areas of knowledge management and business development and can range from participating in innovation strategy groups and developing lawtech and innovation training programs, to organizing networking industry events. Which of these are included in a legal engineer's role will depend on the set-up of the firm's innovation team and whether or not specialized roles for such tasks exist.

What skills should legal engineers have?

To be effective in their role, legal engineers need a skill set that blends sufficient legal knowledge with an understanding of technology. There are different views of how well developed these skills need to be and what additional skills a legal engineer should have. This depends on the structure of the firm and whether further complementing innovations roles exist in the firm, i.e., how many of the various innovation tasks are bundled in the role of the legal engineer.

Among the many skills that are advantageous for a legal engineer to have are:

- Project management;
- Problem solving;
- Creative thinking;
- Commercial awareness; and
- An ability to remain focused on longer-term goals.

Of special importance, however, are legal and technological knowledge, communication skills, and holistic, analytical thinking.

Legal and technological knowledge

The question of the desirable legal and technological knowledge is closely related to the question of which educational background a legal engineer should have.

For many years, it has been discussed that it would be trained lawyers who would develop into individuals with broader skill sets and technological knowledge, often described as the "T-shaped lawyer".[6] As the technological and innovative disruption continues to evolve, I do not believe that all newly created roles – such as the legal engineer – will be performed by lawyers alone. To the contrary, I believe that with the continuous commercialization of the legal sector we will see new specializations, which will eventually be reflected in legal education. In addition, it will be even more important to have highly specialized lawyers who continue to deliver legal excellence. These emerging roles, e.g., legal project manager, legal service process manager, data analyst, and legal engineer will form a symbiosis with lawyers in order to offer excellent and scalable legal services that will drive efficiencies and deliver client demands. Hence, in my view, legal engineers – like many other new experts – do not need to be lawyers, but rather individuals that have an understanding of law and how the legal market and law firms operate, as well as a technological understanding.

The same can be said of the need for an engineering background. It is not uncommon that in start-ups, a legal engineer does have an engineering background and writes code, but this is typically not the case in law firms. In law firms, it is much more important that the legal engineer knows how to grasp and write the requirements, not the code.

Legal engineers should have an overview and understanding of lawtech and the current stage and maturity of the technology, e.g., Natural Language Processing (NLP) in contract analysis, to be able to select the appropriate lawtech for the firm and use case.

Depending on the area of law for which the link between law and technology is supposed to be created, different specific legal and technological expertise is necessary, e.g., in banking law knowledge of blockchain, crypto currencies, and smart contracts is of great advantage.[7]

It is also helpful for the legal engineer to have an understanding of the legal, regulatory, and compliance requirements regarding the implementation of technology, e.g., data protection.

More important than an in-depth legal expertise is some operational knowledge of the law and how lawyers work in different practice groups and how law firms and the legal market function.

Communication

The importance of communication in legal engineering cannot be overstated. Legal engineers constantly need to apply their communication skills to truly understand the requirements at hand, the (underlying) interests, the purpose of the implementation, needs and pain points, and expected results. It is crucial to capture requirements in a way that makes clear which functions must be included and which are nice-to-haves.

Legal engineers need to be bilingual in law and tech terminology and be able to translate the input provided by legal professionals into clear and precise functional and non-functional requirements with accompanying test cases in order to ensure that the actual results align with the expected results.

Clear and transparent communication, especially regarding what lawtech can and cannot deliver, will help to close the expectation gap[8] and result in greater user acceptance. These also apply to managing stakeholder and user expectations regarding their necessary involvement and commitment during the implementation process. The success of a lawtech implementation greatly depends on this commitment, e.g., providing input and test data, giving feedback, and investing time testing the solution.

Holistic, analytical, and agile thinking

Holistic and agile thinking enables legal engineers to be able to see and maintain an overview of the big picture, understand the commercial strategy, and apply their problem solving and project management skills in an agile and flexible manner.

Legal engineers may need to select from a range of project management methodologies and design thinking to align with stakeholder preferences while continuing to promote innovative alternatives.

Analytical and structured thinking is crucial to understanding and analysing business processes, i.e., the way that legal services are provided. Using this analysis, legal engineers can identify potential efficiency gains and propose solutions for their realization.

Does every law firm need legal engineers?

A law firm's need for legal engineers depends on its business and billing model, market strategy, and willingness to make strategic long-term investments. The legal market is continuously changing from a supply-driven market towards a demand-driven market.[9]

One of the key findings of The Law Society's 2019 Lawtech Adoption Research report was that there is an "*increased pressure for firms based in the UK to use or expand the use of lawtech*",[10] mainly driven by a need for greater efficiency. In addition, smaller firms can use the implementation of legal technology to differentiate themselves in their sector and take on larger, more profitable work.[11] Yet, significant barriers to adoption appear to remain, despite the realization that the adoption of legal technology will bring a competitive advantage.[12] Implementing the role of a legal engineer can help to overcome these barriers and drive adoption.

Most law firms' risk analysis will therefore conclude that not investing in innovation and creating these new roles is a greater long-term risk than investing in innovation, which might have an uncertain or delayed RoI. To mitigate the innovation risks, a great number of law firms focus on implementing highly commoditized lawtech.

It may not be the case that the entire firm and all of the practice groups need a legal engineer at the same time, but it is likely that several practice groups within a law firm will greatly benefit from the help of a legal engineer to improve how their legal services are provided.

What do law firms need to create the role of a legal engineer?

To successfully implement the role of legal engineer, it is crucial that they have a productive environment they can operate in, i.e., legal engineers cannot fulfil their role effectively without the necessary structure, culture, and support of the entire firm.

The organizational structure of the firm needs to enable the legal engineer, by creating legal operations or innovation teams, living an innovative mindset, and establishing approval processes. More enablers are clear data protection and professional regulatory compliance guidelines that can be integrated into the lawtech implementation process.

The readiness of the law firm to create these roles mainly depends on two factors – an innovation mindset and an innovation-focused business model.

Innovation mindset

An innovation mindset consists of openness to change, the willingness to question the status quo, and encouragement to think outside the box. For it to flourish, it needs to be embedded in the organizational identity. Most importantly, the cultural reality in which innovation can thrive needs the commitment and support of the partners and both need to be reflected on a practical level.

This means that fee earners as well as service professionals need to be encouraged to be open to new ways of providing legal services and given time in their busy schedules to be active participants in the innovation process. It is only with their experience and input that the legal engineer can thrive and implement lawtech and processes that add the most value. Creative and innovative thinking also needs to be rewarded.

Innovation business model

The business model and commercial strategy of the law firm should include innovation. This means that there should be a dedicated budget for innovation and lawtech.

Law firms have to become more flexible, able to adjust their business and pricing models in order to remain aligned to market demands and opportunities. Growing competition from alternative legal service providers is increasing commercial pressure on traditionally structured law firms. These realignments are a good time to question critically the billable hour, consider alternative fee arrangements, and think about whether the partnership model is the right structure to support the firm's innovation strategy.

The initial investment required to align a firm's business model with market demands is relatively large. Commercial pressure is likely not equally high on all practice groups and business areas; hence, it may be preferable to focus on one or two high priority practice groups first and apply it to further business areas at a later point.

Summary

Legal engineers operate at the intersection of law, people, technology, and process. Their role mainly focuses on the implementation of lawtech and its application to legal services. Among the most important skills are legal and technological knowledge and communication skills.

Individuals interested in becoming legal engineers should look out for university programs that include courses on legal technology and/or legal operations. In addition, there are a number of (online) events and courses that offer an introduction and overview on the topic of digital innovation in law. When joining a law firm, they should pay special attention to the innovation and operational structure within the law firm and ask how the firm defines the role, to make sure it is in line with their interests and skills.

Legal engineers greatly depend on a supportive and enabling innovation structure within the law firm to realize their potential. To be able to keep up with the ever-evolving demand-driven market, every law firm should consider implementing this role and should make sure its mindset and innovation budget matches its ambition.

References

1. Omar Salah, *Sukuk Structures: Legal Engineering Under Dutch Law*, Eleven International Publishing, 2014.
2. Doreen McBarnet, *Financial Engineering or Legal Engineering? Legal Work, Legal Integrity and the Banking Crisis*, University of Edinburgh School of Law Working Paper No. 2010/2, 2010. Retrieved 19 February 2022, from https://ssrn.com/abstract=1546486.
3. Jake Goldenfein and Andrea Leiter, *Legal Engineering on the Blockchain: 'Smart Contracts' as Legal Conduct*, 2018. Retrieved 19 February 2022, from https://ssrn.com/abstract=3176363.
4. Legal engineering law firms aim to build legal solutions at the interface of tech, data and the law; *Lawtech Adoption Research Report*, The Law Society, 2019, p43. Retrieved 19 February 2022, from www.lawsociety.org.uk/topics/research/lawtech-adoption-report.
5. *Lawtech Adoption Research Report*, The Law Society, 2019, p5. Retrieved 19 February 2022, from www.lawsociety.org.uk/topics/research/lawtech-adoption-report.
6. Elaine Mak, *The T-shaped Lawyer and Beyond. Rethinking Legal Professionalism and Legal Education for Contemporary Societies*, Inaugural Lecture for the Chair of Jurisprudence at Utrecht University, delivered on 19 June 2017, p.1. Retrieved 18 February 2022, from https://www.researchgate.net/publication/331022253_The_T-shaped_Lawyer_and_Beyond_Rethinking_legal_professionalism_and_legal_education_for_contemporary_societies.

7. Alexandre Cavalcanti Andrade de Araújo, *Internet and New Technologies Law: Perspectives and Challenges*, Nomos Verlagsgesellschaft mbH & Co. KG, 2021, pp.38-41.
8. See section on Implementation of procured technology.
9. Ron Dolin and Thomas Buley, *Legal Informatics*, Cambridge University Press, 2021, p.453.
10. *Lawtech Adoption Research report*, The Law Society, 2019. Retrieved 19 February 2022, from www.lawsociety.org.uk/topics/research/lawtech-adoption-report.
11. *Ibid*, p.19.
12. *Ibid*, p.8.

Chapter 12: The emerging world of ESG

By Claire Shasha, lawyer and ESG advocate

What is ESG?

ESG is everywhere. Everyone from regulators and companies to customers around the globe are talking about it. COP26 shone a spotlight on the ever-increasing effects of climate change on the world, and reports such as the 2022 IPCC[1] report highlighted that approximately 3.3 to 3.6 billion people live in contexts that are highly vulnerable to climate change, with the window of opportunity to tackle climate change rapidly narrowing. In addition, the rise of social justice movements such as Black Lives Matter and #MeToo have highlighted the social inadequacies that the world still needs to address.

ESG as a term originated in the financial sector as a way for potential investors to measure the behavior and performance of a company against pre-defined environmental, social, and governance goals. It is now used more widely as an umbrella term to cover multiple environmental, social, and governance factors and has in the main replaced Corporate Social Responsibility as the most used term.

The E is for Environment and includes greenhouse gas emissions such as carbon, pollution and waste, biodiversity, and climate change impact. The S stands for Social and addresses the relationship a company has with its employees, stakeholders, and the communities in which it does business. It encompasses labor relations, modern slavery and human rights, diversity and inclusion (D&I) including equal pay, and employee welfare including health and safety. The G is for Governance and covers the systems and controls needed for a company to govern itself, ensuring the obligations of the law and its stakeholders' needs are met.

The area of ESG is complex and evolving, without fixed boundaries. It is beyond the scope of this chapter to delve into each ESG topic area in depth. This chapter will look at the key trends emerging and how individual lawyers, law firms, and in-house legal teams can best position themselves in this new and emerging area.

Emerging trends

The rise of regulation and reporting

A key driver of the rise in prominence of ESG has been the increase in legislation and regulation and with it a rise in reporting requirements. The UK government announced that, from April 2022, more companies will be required to disclose their climate-related risks and opportunities in line with Taskforce on Climate-related Financial Disclosures (TCFD) recommendations. The EU is leading the way in ESG disclosure regimes. Its Sustainable Finance Disclosure Regulation sets out harmonized rules for financial market participation related to the transparency of sustainable risk. In addition, the European Commission's Corporate Sustainability Reporting Directive (CSRD) comes into effect in December 2022. It will replace and strengthen the existing requirements, capturing more companies, and extending the reporting requirements. Elsewhere, the International Financial Reporting Standards Foundation (IFRS) has announced the formation of the International Sustainability Standards Board (ISSB) tasked with developing mandatory corporate ESG disclosures. Given IFRS's global reach of its accounting standards, the ISSB could have a wide impact globally. Companies will need to keep on top of their changing obligations.

Supply chain collaboration

Companies pledging to follow the Science Based Targets initiative (SBTi) must significantly cut their scope 1, 2 and 3 emissions,[2] requiring an assessment of all supplier emissions. Collaboration will be key. Companies will need to reframe their suppliers as stakeholders and work with them to share knowledge and create innovative solutions to reach their targets. For example, the water company Anglian Water partnered with OastHouse to use the heat generated by wastewater from water plants to heat huge greenhouses, capable of producing 12 percent of the UK's tomatoes with a 75 percent reduction in carbon footprint.[3] Due diligence on supply chains will also be crucial for companies. In February 2022, the European Commission presented a directive on corporate sustainability due diligence, the first-ever set of EU-wide rules relating to companies' supply chains.[4] If enacted, companies will be required to identify and, where necessary, prevent adverse impacts of their activities on the environment and on human rights.

The green consumer

There has been increased pressure from consumers and stakeholders on companies to become more sustainable. Consumers have become more concerned about climate change and where and how products are produced. Websites such as GoodOnYou are emerging that rank fashion brands on their sustainability credentials.[5] A report by Bupa[6] also found that 31 percent of Generation Z would turn down a role in companies with poor ESG credentials. In recent years there has also been pressure from institutional investors, such as pension funds and asset managers, who are looking at long-term sustainability for their investments. They are using their power to attach ESG conditions to their investment criteria and more recently influencing behavior through their voting rights. Without improving their ESG credentials, companies risk a negative impact on not only their reputation but also their balance sheet.

Risky business

The assessment and mitigation of risk will be essential. Companies will need to quantify the risk, both in terms of their effect on the environment but also how climate change will affect the company's sustainability in the future. A report by Munich Re[7] found that natural disasters destroyed assets totaling US$280bn in 2021, an increase of 33 percent from the previous year. Balancing a company's commercial needs and its reputational risk is increasingly important. The fashion brand Boohoo is still suffering reputational damage from 2019, when poor pay and working conditions were exposed in one of its UK factories.[8] As such, one of the biggest reputational risks will be the disconnect between what a company says and what it is doing, with "greenwashing" becoming a focus for regulators, including the UK's Financial Conduct Authority. Litigation risk is also on the increase. Globally, the cumulative number of climate change-related cases has more than doubled since 2015[9] and large cases such as *Milieudefensie et al. v. Royal Dutch Shell plc* (2019) have highlighted the need to properly assess a company's exposure to litigation risk.

ESG specific roles in the legal sector

A 2022 report by LinkedIn[10] paints a worrying picture of the green skills gaps the business world is currently facing, noting that there is currently not the green skillset to deliver the green transition. The report found that together green[11] and greening jobs[12] still only account for ten percent of hiring in 2021, while non-green jobs dominated at 50 percent. While some countries went against the trend, the report found that the legal sector across the globe has one of the lowest green skills usages. This position is changing, and the trend shows lawyers are transitioning into green/greening jobs faster than they are into non-green jobs.

While there has been a rise in ESG specific roles outside of law, ESG is still very much an emerging area of expertise within the legal profession and ESG service offerings are at a relatively early stage of development across the legal industry.

Private practice

The larger UK and international law firms have started to rebrand themselves and include "sustainability" as a new pillar within their business models. There are now partner roles specifically orientated towards ESG, ranging from heads of ESG and sustainability through to more specific environmental roles such as head of environment and climate change. These roles head up the new sustainability pillar for the firms and provide the lead for client-facing advice in the ESG space. Most of these positions sit alongside existing roles heading up traditional function areas within the firm.

As well as these specific roles, law firms are bringing together other lawyers from various departments and qualification levels to form their client-facing ESG specialist team. While this might be happening within the top firms, not all law firms have sought the opportunity to rebrand themselves. The 2021 Stellar Performance report by Thomas Reuters found that although 85 percent of respondents said they were seeing their clients' businesses increasingly focused on ESG issues, only just over half were proactively talking to their clients about how they could support and advise them.[13]

All the partners I spoke to when preparing this chapter ended up involved in ESG through a combination of interest in and desire to be proactive in the ESG space, synergies with their existing practice areas, and from taking on matters that had an element of ESG contained within them. As a partner from Pinsent Masons noted, "Once you start advising on an ESG matter you start to build a reputation as the ESG expert and naturally get involved in more ESG deals". Through their involvement and emerging ESG reputation, partners have often been asked to lead their firms in delivering their own internal ESG targets and aims, with some leading their firm's race for a carbon neutral program and their D&I strategy.

For those wishing to become solely focused on environmental matters, there are also specialist law firms that deal with climate matters. For example, ClientEarth aims to use the law to change the system through implementing and enforcing the law, advising on policies and training the legal profession.[14]

In-house

The 2022 annual global review of Chief Legal Officers (CLOs) by the Association of Corporate Counsel found an increase in the focus of ESG issues for lawyers.[15] The main concentration of respondents was in the US (67 percent), and the survey found that CLOs are getting more involved in ESG and CSR issues with 24 percent of CLOs declaring that they now oversee this function, an increase of nine percent from the previous year.

This trend may vary by company with many creating separate function areas to focus on ESG and CSR, with in-house legal teams lending support and expertise where needed. Some companies have posted positions for senior counsel responsible for the legal aspects of sustainability and ESG but these are not yet common in the UK. However, ESG touches all areas of the business and therefore all legal teams will need to understand ESG issues and risks and be able to advise on how to mitigate those risks.

What can you do to pivot?

ESG will increasingly become a focus for companies of all sizes. For lawyers wishing to pivot their careers into this area there are several steps they can take.

Upskill

Lawyers must upskill themselves on the technical side. As with all disciplines, ESG has its own terminology and language and a substantial array of legislation, regulation, standards, and guidance.

There are now a range of short- and long-term courses available. The University of Cambridge and the CFA Society UK both provide short online courses covering topics such as ESG finance, business sustainability, and ESG investing. Smith School of Enterprise and the Environment, together with University of Oxford, provides a short course on law and sustainability. Although the cost of these courses can be up to £2,500, they may be a worthwhile investment as more recruiters and companies look for tangible experience and technical knowledge of sustainability.[16]

There is a wealth of publicly available information available for lawyers to review. Many large law firms and consultancies have excellent reports and bulletins on ESG topic areas. Podcasts can be another source of insightful ESG discussions. For example, Ashurst runs an extremely informative podcast[17] as does Herbert Smith Freehills[18] and consulting firms like EY[19] and PWC,[20] to name a few. Joining ESG and sustainability groups on LinkedIn and getting invited to seminars and conferences are other easy ways in which to upskill yourself.

Organizations such as The Chancery Lane Project (TCLP) have some excellent resources and toolkits for lawyers. TCLP has created a bank of draft clauses organized by sector and practice area that aim to help lawyers align their companies' contracts to their net zero carbon emissions. By reading these draft clauses, lawyers will be able to educate themselves on areas of concern and what issues need to be addressed and how. TCLP also produces updates and newsletters that will help subscribers keep up to date.

ESG is an exciting opportunity for junior lawyers to step up and take a leading role. It is an emerging area within the legal sector where there is the opportunity to develop their careers and gain greater exposure to senior leaders at a greater rate than in more traditional sectors.

Get involved

In-house lawyers are in a unique position of influence within a company, often sitting at the top on boards and committees and having an unrivalled oversight of the business. As such, general counsel and senior lawyers are in a perfect position to proactively get involved with the company's ESG agenda. Although more junior lawyers may not have this level of influence, they can advocate a business case for how the legal team can better support the company with its ESG goals.

Lawyers have key skills that companies will need to leverage if they are to set and achieve their ESG goals. They can digest large amounts of complex information and distil it into practical advice and can critically assess risk, balancing a company's legal obligations, its commercial needs, and reputational risks. As noted, companies currently face notable reputational risk arising from a disconnect between what it says and what it does on ESG. Lawyers can help companies critically assess whether the language used in a company's statements amounts to legally binding representations or commitments, and can undertake operational and contract reviews to test for areas of vulnerability to green litigation.

All business relationships center around legal contracts. The supply chain is a key ESG issue for companies to address and lawyers should review all supplier contracts and work with the suppliers to negotiate clauses that will help both parties to achieve their net zero targets. Issues such as liabilities will be pivotal. Pushing liability and more obligations down the supply chain may mean suppliers are not able to comply and may create an unfair burden on them. Collaboration is key and lawyers can help facilitate this. Lawyers can also work with procurement teams to build new due diligence supplier questionnaires to help identify gaps in the supply chain.

Other areas of possible proactive focus are policy reviews to ensure they are aligned to the company's ESG agenda and the changing legislative landscape, advising on the tricky issue of director remuneration and whether ESG targets can be pegged to pay, and training directors and the business on legal duties and ESG obligations. Lawyers may also be able to help companies achieve a recognized ESG certification such as becoming a B Corp company.

In-house lawyers can also support themselves by becoming part of groups such as Lawyers for Net Zero whose aims are to help in-house legal teams empower change within their companies and build agency and momentum.[21] By joining such communities, lawyers can gain support from other lawyers and share knowledge of leading practices and thought leadership.

While I have focused this sub-section on in-house lawyers, private practice lawyers can think about how these issues affect their own clients and proactively advise accordingly.

Network

Networking is crucial to career development, especially when thinking of pivoting into a different area. Think about who in your organization is responsible for achieving the ESG targets and ask what they are doing and how they became involved in ESG. Find out what is happening within your company or law firm and think of ways you and the wider legal team can offer them support with their ESG aims. Are there possibilities of short-term or long-term secondments into the ESG teams to gain real experience and knowledge in these areas?

Look to your external contacts. Does anyone in your network work in this area or work for companies that are strong in ESG actions that you can contact? Connect with ESG or sustainability groups and forums. The more you connect to people, the more opportunities you create and the more knowledge you will gain in this area.

Volunteer

Volunteering is a great way to gain experience, make an impact, expand your network, and potentially open up opportunities. There is a plethora of charities and organizations that support actions on the environmental and social front that would be open to any volunteering support. TCLP often have opportunities to volunteer and get involved.

There may also be opportunities within your own organization. At Bupa, a grassroots D&I employee forum was created by a handful of employees with a passion for diversity. Can you join similar groups in your company or start an initiative yourself? In larger companies you may be able to get involved with community foundations supporting the local community. These will provide opportunities to gain experience developing and driving forward a company's "social" aims, while benefiting the employees, business, and community as a whole.

Join a board or committee

Lastly, getting onto a board or committee is a good way to be a part of a company's strategic discussions on ESG. Even small companies will need to set targets and actions to become more sustainable and will value support and advice from lawyers. At this level you can have a strong influence over the company and be able to focus attention on the ESG agenda. When thinking about board or committee service, however, you will need to think carefully about how much time realistically you will be able to give, bearing in mind the flexibility that might be needed in certain periods. This will help you evaluate what boards or committees you would be best suited to join.

Conclusion

ESG is still a developing area but one that will only grow in significance. Lawyers with their skill sets and unique position within companies are perfectly placed to become a proactive force in helping companies to achieve their ESG goals. It is, therefore, a perfect time to rebrand and pivot one's career to being an ESG lawyer.

References

1. The Intergovernmental Panel on Climate Change (2022), "Climate change: a threat to human wellbeing and health of the planet": www.ipcc.ch/2022/02/28/pr-wgii-ar6/.
2. Defined by Greenhouse Gas (GHG) Protocol.
3. www.lowcarbonfarming.co.uk/
4. www.ec.europa.eu/commission/presscorner/detail/en/ip_22_1145
5. www.goodonyou.eco
6. Bupa (2022), "Gen Z seek ethical workplaces as environmental health burden bites": www.bupa.com/news/press-releases/2022/gen-z-seek-ethical-workplaces-as-environ-mental-health-burden-bites.

7. Munich Re (2022), "Hurricanes, cold waves, tornadoes: Weather disasters in USA dominate natural disaster losses in 2021": www.munichre.com/en/company/media-relations/media-information-and-corporate-news/media-information/2022/natural-disaster-losses-2021.html.
8. *The Times* (10 December 2021), "Boohoo investors are still in tears over retailer's ethical credentials": www.thetimes.co.uk/article/boohoo-still-under-scrutiny-from-investors-over-ethical-credentials-n8vkptckm.
9. J Setzer and C Higham (2021), "Global trends in climate change litigation: 2021 snapshot", London: Grantham Research Institute on Climate Change and the Environment and Centre for Climate Change Economics and Policy, London School of Economics and Political Science: www.lse.ac.uk/granthaminstitute/wp-content/uploads/2021/07/Global-trends-in-climate-change-litigation_2021-snapshot.pdf.
10. LinkedIn (2022), Global Green Skills Report 2022: https://economicgraph.linkedin.com/content/dam/me/economicgraph/en-us/global-green-skills-report/global-green-skills-report-pdf/li-green-economy-report-2022.pdf.
11. Defined in the report as those jobs that cannot be performed without extensive knowledge of green skills.
12. Defined in the report as those jobs that can be performed without green skills, but typically require some green skills.
13. Thomas Reuters (2021), Stellar Performance: Skills and Progression Mid-Year Survey: www.thomsonreuters.com/en-us/posts/wp-content/uploads/sites/20/2021/11/Standout-Lawyers-2021_LawFirms_FINAL-web.pdf.
14. www.clientearth.org/
15. Association of Corporate Counsel (2022), 2022 Chief Legal Officers Survey: www.acc.com/clo2022.
16. These represent a sample of courses available and are not an endorsement or recommendation of the quality or suitability of the course by the author.
17. ESG Matters @Ashursts.
18. ESG Transformation Conversation Series.
19. EY: Sustainability Matters.
20. Episodes samples: PWC: Risk and Regulation Rundown; PWC IFRS: Talks and PWC: Business in Focus.
21. www.lawyersfornetzero.com

Chapter 13: Hyperspecialization: how the Digital Revolution will lead to new legal careers

By Rebecca Holdredge, director of knowledge management, Levenfeld Pearlstein

If you've ever worked with a software company, you've probably noticed the plethora of different titles of the people you interact with. There are the customer success managers, account executives, solution architects, support specialists, systems analysts, and project managers, and that list doesn't even include the software developers! However, if you've worked with a law firm, you may have interacted with a lawyer, possibly a paralegal, but that's probably about it. Why is it that law firms don't have specific roles like customer success managers and account executives like software companies? The answer is because, as industries mature, what were once generalist roles get broken into specialized and even hyperspecialized roles, with each new role more streamlined and operating more efficiently than the previous generalist role. And the reason the variety of roles exist in the technology industry (as compared to the legal industry) is because the software industry is further along and more mature in its digital transformation journey than the legal industry. As the legal industry continues its digital transformation, firms will employ fewer generalists, and the traditional attorney role will be broken down into more and more specialized roles, providing a variety of new legal careers.

The purpose of this chapter is to show that as the legal industry continues through the Digital Revolution, just like the technology industry, hyperspecialization will occur, which will result in a huge increase in the number of alternative legal careers (i.e., non-practicing roles for those with law degrees). The chapter begins by describing the Digital Revolution and how the legal industry is finally starting to see this digital transformation and what is fueling the increased rate of change. It then goes on to describe the concept of hyperspecialization and why it occurs in maturing industries. Finally, the chapter lays out how the Digital Revolution will result in a variety of new, hyperspecialized roles in the legal industry and examples of these new legal careers.

The Digital Revolution: impact on the legal industry

Modern civilization is currently witnessing its fourth major revolution, the Digital Revolution, which, by most accounts, began in the 1980s with the advent of the internet. During each of these transformational periods, society has been forced to rethink how people work together, live together, and communicate with each other. Change has not been optional. Businesses that refuse to evolve get left behind. Just imagine a manufacturer during the Industrial Revolution that refused to transition from hand production methods to a mechanized factory – most likely a distant memory as it had little chance of survival.

Even knowing change is underway and companies must innovate to survive, the legal industry has been slow to adapt to the Digital Revolution. As other industries have adopted new digital technologies and processes to meet client demands, law firms have watched from afar, conservatively adopting changes once they've been thoroughly vetted. Given the profession focuses on eliminating risk and has no tolerance for failure, it is hardly surprising the industry is reluctant to embrace disruptive changes, even when they are imperative. However, avoiding the Digital Revolution is no longer an option for law firms as new technologies and new competition have forced firms to rethink the way day-to-day business is done. Tech-savvy clients and entrepreneurial young attorneys are pressuring firms to digitize their operations, wanting to ensure key decisions, actions, and processes are strongly influenced by data-driven insights, rather than by human intuition. While once lawyers had little competition for their services, now, fueled by new technologies, competition comes from multiple directions, with companies like the Big Four accounting firms, start-ups, legal technology companies (e.g., Legal Zoom), and consulting companies all chipping away at tasks that were once considered traditional legal services (e.g., contract management, eDiscovery, document automation). Even within firms, tech-savvy attorneys with nontraditional skills and backgrounds (e.g., coding, software development, project management, data science, analytics) are in higher demand. Digital processes and data-driven insights have become the cornerstones of the current revolution and law firms need to harness the power of technology to stand a chance of survival.

In addition to new technologies, the COVID-19 pandemic highlighted the benefits of being data-driven and tech-savvy, and thus accelerated law firms' need for a speedy digital transformation. In 2020, law firms suddenly and unexpectedly needed to switch to remote work almost overnight and adopting new technology was the only way to continue client services. The fancy offices on the top floors of the busiest cities, that were once a firm's sign of prestige, became essentially worthless. Clients wanted speed and efficiency – practical solutions as quickly as possible. Signs of prestige became firms that could quickly adopt new technologies (e.g., replacing in-person meetings with video calls, replacing phone calls with text messages). Firms' online presence became more important than their physical presence and things like online billing and client portals became necessities. When it became apparent how quickly firms were able to change when forced, they began to better understand the opportunities that technology could provide to improve productivity, enhancing both employees' lives and client relationships.

While the economy's digital transformation generally has aided the transition to hyperspecialization, the new remote workforce, a demand for work–life balance, and the gig economy are accelerating this transition. The traditional associate-to-partnership model has been evolving over the last few decades to keep law firms' profits per partner (PPP) metrics competitive (i.e., a higher non-partner to partner ratio helps increase the PPP calculation). One way to maximize the utility of the partners that remain is requiring more standardization, being able to provide clients with similar services with less effort, which can be done with the use of boilerplate documents and knowledge management systems. In addition, associate turnover rates have reached almost 25 percent,[1] which means the chance that an associate makes partner at the firm where they started their career may now be in the single digits. Fewer and fewer associates are lured to Big Law with the hopes that if they put in grueling hours for eight to ten years, they will make partner. Many new attorneys are looking for roles doing interesting work with flexible schedules, with the partnership track no longer as attractive as it once was. With the trend of working from home here to stay and a current workforce with a laser focus on work–life balance, firms that were once reluctant to enter the Digital Revolution are now aware of how digital information and processes can enable them to drive business growth and attract and retain top talent.

While strongly influenced by technology, the real essence of digital transformation is modernizing how businesses operate, streamlining operations, adopting new tools, with the goal of delivering more value to clients. Digitizing operations is just the new technology that helps businesses achieve those objectives. There are some signs that firms are making headway – many firms are starting to identify and implement new processes and technologies that increase productivity and deliver a more rewarding client experience. Firms further along in their digital transformation journey have invested in intelligent workflows, user interface/user experience (UI/UX), product design, no-code tools, document automation, and natural language processing/artificial intelligence tools. To successfully survive, firms must reevaluate every aspect of how they operate to add value and provide an enhanced customer experience.

The Digital Revolution: digital maturity leads to hyperspecialized roles

In Adam Smith's *The Wealth of Nations*,[2] written at the beginning of the Industrial Revolution, he described the economic concept of division of labor through "specialization". He theorized that as companies grew and hired more workers, physical tasks could be divided among a group of workers so each worker could focus on a lesser number of tasks, thus becoming more skilled and faster at their assigned tasks. Like the assembly line, the goal of specialization is ultimately to create more efficient, and thus profitable, operations. Smith provides an example of workers in a pin factory, describing how one job could be transformed into 18 separate tasks. If one worker had to perform all 18 tasks, he estimated that worker could produce no more than 20 pins in one day. However, if those 18 tasks were divided among a group of workers, each specializing in one or two of the pin-making operations, he estimated they would be able to work more efficiently and could produce up to 4,800 pins per day.

A 2011 *Harvard Business Review* article[3] went one step further to show a rise in technology goes hand-in-hand with specialization by outlining how Adam Smith's division of labor concept that transformed physical work during the Industrial Revolution could be taken to the next level to predict how knowledge work (i.e., professional services) would be transformed during the Digital Revolution. The article explains that as companies continue to adopt new technologies and look for additional ways to maintain profitability, they will begin to enter the era of "hyperspecialization", a more extreme scenario where roles are divided into smaller and smaller tasks, requiring even more highly specialized professionals. Hyperspecialization can improve both quality and efficiency of work product because (1) more work is done by people who are good at it, and (2) since related tasks can be assigned to multiple people, they can be accomplished in parallel (instead of one person having to do each task serially). Transitioning to these specialized roles can also improve morale, as it becomes easier for workers to mix-and-match different expert skills into their ideal job and creates a more autonomous and flexible work environment. Just as physical laborers transitioned from generalist to specialist roles during the Industrial Revolution, professional services should also begin to transition from generalist to specialist knowledge roles during the Digital Revolution.

While the legal industry has already seen some degree of specialization, as evidenced by the creation of more and more niche practice areas (think craft beverage, blockchain, or mortuary law), most lawyers remain generalists in how they operate their practice day-to-day. We can look to the software industry as an example of this hyperspecialization concept and a foreshadow of what might be on the horizon for the legal industry. What was once a software developer role has now been divided into many sub-roles: data architect, systems engineer, and cybersecurity specialist. Projects that used to be self-managed are now managed by dedicated project management teams. Instead of looking to the creative person on the team to come up with the next product, entire Research and Development teams are tasked with determining what clients might want next. Product design and user experience (UX) are now specific disciplines instead of nice-to-have qualities. With hyperspecialists, more qualified people can handle these tasks, delivering faster and higher quality results.

Now imagine if a lawyer's role was broken down into each unique sub-task. While certain aspects of the job immediately come to mind (e.g., legal research and writing, negotiation and mediation, or arguing cases in court), there are numerous other facets to an attorney's job that can be tasked out to specialists (e.g., marketing/sales, client relationship management, pricing, billing, recruiting, training, project management, innovation, public speaking, strategic planning). While this division of labor may sound far-fetched to some current practicing attorneys, looking at the transformation of the technology industry over the last 20 years should indicate that change is on the horizon. Now, layer on brand new technology available today and what related services clients might be looking to their law firm to provide, and you can image a whole host of other areas where new specialized roles (i.e., new alternative legal careers) could (and in some cases have been seen to) emerge, such as legal operations, contract management, innovation, product sales, quality assurance, eDiscovery, knowledge management, data science, program management, information governance… the list goes on and on.

Hyperspecialization example

One example of specialization in the legal industry is legal operations, which is a newer field where business professionals use a combination of business processes and activities – such as strategic planning, financial management, project management, and technology expertise – to streamline legal work and enable legal professionals to focus on providing legal advice. It is essential business support for the legal function. Now, in reality, as long as there have been lawyers, there has been legal operations (whether done by the attorney themselves or support staff), but now it's a well-defined multi-disciplinary field that people can seek out proactively as a career, instead of it being just one aspect of a larger role. In the past few decades, this function has matured and gained more adoption and the scope and complexity of the role has increased. Industry organizations, like the Corporate Legal Operations Consortium (CLOC), have even published a "maturity model",[4] helping assess the effectiveness of their legal operations functions and what additional capabilities need to be acquired to improve performance. As this function matures, we start experiencing the next logical step: specialization within legal operations – or hyperspecialization.

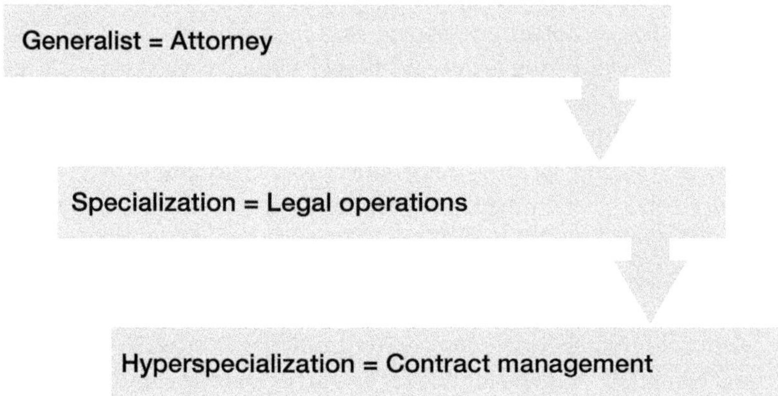

Hyperspecialization can be seen in the legal industry in the area of contract management (a subset of legal operations) focused specifically on creating, executing, and storing contracts. Businesses enter a variety of contracts daily, which traditionally have been drafted, negotiated, reviewed, and executed with the help of a corporate attorney. As new technologies emerge that allow for faster and easier contract drafting and execution (e.g., document automation, electronic signature capture), businesses are now entering more contracts than ever before. The sheer volume of contracts has quickly become overwhelming and difficult for attorneys to maintain, and given their hourly rate and client's cost sensitivities, the contract operations professional was born. Given the importance of contracts to a company – the basis of every legal right and obligation and dictates much of what happens within a company – shouldn't there be a dedicated role for such a critical function? These professionals understand the contract lifecycle, can draft standard contracts from templates, serve as the central repository for all contracts, maintain the database of each document's features, establish appropriate approval workflows, and alert the attorney when the need arises. All of this can be done by a professional that specializes in just the one task of contract management and accomplished at a lower price point than traditional legal work. This is just one instance of how Adam Smith's pin factory example can now be applied to the legal industry.

Conclusion

As new technologies are introduced, companies become more profitable and industries become more competitive, specialization is used to reduce costs and maintain profitability. This concept of role specialization, where employees focus on one skill to become more efficient at it, is a sign of an industry's maturity. Mature industries can be identified by having even more specialized, or "hyperspecialized", roles. We've already started to see this concept of specialization increase the availability of alternative legal careers, or non-traditional jobs for people with a legal background. Roles like pricing, knowledge management (KM), and legal project management (LPM), which were once rolled into the generalist attorney role, are now separate career paths. Ultimately, as hyperspecialization of the legal industry occurs, the attorney's role will continue to be broken down into smaller and smaller pieces, increasing the availability and need for alternative legal careers, such as sales, customer success, and project management, as well as roles that will be available in ten years that do not even exist now. A combination of digital transformation, new competition, and a new remote workforce that demands a different work–life balance ensures that hyperspecialization of the legal industry is not a fad that will soon disappear.

References

1. Roy Strom, "Record Salaries Aren't Stopping Associate Turnover 'Crisis' (1)." *Bloomberg Law*, 13 January 2022: https://news.bloomberglaw.com/business-and-practice/record-salaries-arent-stopping-associate-turnover-crisis. Accessed 1 April 2022.
2. Adam Smith, *An Inquiry into the Nature and Causes of the Wealth of Nations* (Cannan ed.), vol. 1. Methuen, 1776.

3. T.W. Malone, R.J. Laubacher and T. Johns, “The Big Idea: The Age of Hyperspecialization”, *Harvard Business Review* 89(7-8): 56-65. July 2011. https://hbr.org/2011/07/the-big-idea-the-age-of-hyperspecialization. Accessed 1 April 2022.
4. Corporate Legal Operations Consortium, *What is Legal Operations?* Tools, Guides and Templates for the Legal Operations Professional, October 2019. https://cloc.org/wp-content/uploads/2019/10/What-is-Legal-Ops_Oct2019-FINAL.pdf. Accessed 1 April 2022.

About Globe Law and Business

Globe Law and Business was established in 2005. From the very beginning, we set out to create law books which are sufficiently high level to be of real use to the experienced professional, yet still accessible and easy to navigate. Most of our authors are drawn from Magic Circle and other top commercial firms, both in the UK and internationally.

Our titles are carefully produced, with the utmost attention paid to editorial, design and production processes. We hope this results in high-quality publications that are easy to read, and a pleasure to own. Our titles are also available as ebooks, which are compatible with most desktop, laptop and tablet devices. In 2018 we expanded our portfolio to include journals and Special Reports, available both digitally and in hard copy format, and produced to the same high standards as our books.

In the spring of 2021, we were very pleased to announce the start of a new chapter for Globe Law and Business following the acquisition of law books under the imprint Ark Publishing. We are very much looking forward to working with our new Ark authors, many of whom are well known to us, to further developing the law firm management list, and to welcoming our new Ark customers.

We'd very much like to hear from you with your thoughts and ideas for improving what we offer. Please do feel free to email me at sian@globelawandbusiness.com with your views.

Sian O'Neill
Managing director
Globe Law and Business
www.globelawandbusiness.com

www.ingramcontent.com/pod-product-compliance
Ingram Content Group UK Ltd.
Pitfield, Milton Keynes, MK11 3LW, UK
UKHW021849150926
8657IPUK00005B/156